Transcriptions • Lessons • Bios • Photos

25 GREAT CLASSIC ROCK GUITAR SOLOS

D1235737

Featuring Legends of Lead Guitar, Including Jimmy Page, Eric Clapton, Eddie Van Halen, Jeff Beck, Carlos Santana, Duane Allman, Tony Iommi, David Gilmour, and Many More

by Dave Rubin

ALSO AVAILABLE:

 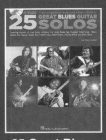 

25 Great Guitar Solos
HL00699721

25 Great Blues Guitar Solos
HL00699790

25 Great Country Guitar Solos
HL00699926

Jimmy Page cover photo © Photofest

Duane Allman cover photo by Amalie R. Rothchild

Eddie Van Halen, David Gilmour, and Eric Clapton cover photos © Retna Ltd.

Tony Iommi cover photo by Marty Temme

ISBN 978-1-4234-6829-5

HAL•LEONARD®
CORPORATION

7777 W. BLUEMOUND RD. P.O. BOX 13819 MILWAUKEE, WI 53213

Visit Hal Leonard Online at
www.halleonard.com

Preface

Rock guitar solos have evolved significantly over time. In the "stone age" of the fifties, they often served merely as an "instrumental break" from the vocals; by the "stoned age" of the sixties, however, they sometimes seemed the whole point of the exercise. Even back then, however, the difference was always in the songs with the closest lineage to the blues. Beginning with Chuck Berry and the raucous, howling highway sound of his grinding solo on "Maybellene" in 1955, a freedom to improvise and express joy, anger, lust, menace, or just sheer rebellion for the hell of it became the province of those players willing to test their mettle (metal?) and chops.

It's a fairly straight shot from Chuck to the Kingsmen in the Northwest in the early sixties and their primal, iconic garage rock version of "Louie Louie" (1963) featuring lead guitarist Mike Mitchell. In England, Jeff Beck was helping to create psychedelic music in the Yardbirds by filtering the blues through Les Paul and rockabilly music, and his wildly creative chops produced the swinging and humorous "Jeff's Boogie" in 1966. His predecessor in the 'birds, Eric Clapton, would advance the cause of heavy blues rock in Cream during the late sixties with dramatic blues rock like the monolithic "White Room" in 1968. A year later in the U.S., a band from northern California led by the exceptionally talented singer/songwriter/guitarist John Fogerty combined country blues with country, folk, and rockabilly music to create a dazzling string of hit singles. "Born on the Bayou," the flipside of the future wedding band staple "Proud Mary," captured a Southern ambience not present in British blues rock. Also in 1969, Mexico-born Carlos Santana in the San Francisco area found yet another way to combine the blues with a new genre in the celebratory Latin rock of "Soul Sacrifice" that he had performed that summer at the landmark Woodstock festival in upstate New York. John Lennon likely thought himself the "bluesiest" of the Beatles, that most eclectic and imaginative of sixties bands, but George Harrison and Paul McCartney joined him in trading funky blues rock solos during their crunching jam on "The End" in 1969 that actually marked the "end" for the Beatles with *Abbey Road*. Led Zeppelin, their polar opposites led by the brilliant tone king Jimmy Page, gave a nod to a passel of blues classics with their original composition "The Lemon Song" on their second release in 1969. That same watershed year, an authentic American blues group from the South, the Allman Brothers Band featuring Duane Allman and Dicky Betts, included the ultimate encore tune of "Whipping Post" on their debut album.

The seventies started off showing no let up in creativity regarding blues influenced rock. Mountain, with the physically "mountainous" lead guitarist Leslie West, paid props to the "Mississippi Queen" in 1970. Across the "big pond," heavy metal avatars Black Sabbath with guitarist Tony Iommi were feeling rather "Paranoid" in 1971, while Deep Purple with the "Dark Knight" Richie Blackmore smoldered with "Smoke on the Water" in 1972. At the same time stateside, the jazz-bopping Steely Dan, with a rotating cast of top session guitarists, recorded the fast shuffling "Reeling in the Years" with studio cat Elliot Randall spinning fluid lines. David Gilmour and the second incarnation of Pink Floyd used "Money" in 1973 to make a major musical statement in England, while the pride of Ohio,

Joe Walsh, let loose with his best slide work to date on the dramatic and slow shuffling "Rocky Mountain Way." Concurrently, the Dutch band Golden Earring, featuring George Kooymans, was filling the airwaves with their own shuffling "Radar Love." That same banner year, Rick Derringer, following a stint with bluesman Johnny and then Edgar Winter, released the boogying "Rock and Roll Hoochie Koo" on his solo debut.

Boston's finest, Aerosmith, with guitar-slinging session cats Steve Hunter and Dick Wagner subbing for lead guitarist Joe Perry, let loose their steaming version of "Train Kept A-Rollin'" in 1974. Their epic production built on the Yardbirds take from 1965 with Jeff Beck, who in turn had been influenced by the Rock and Roll Trio and their 1956 version of Tiny Bradshaw's original from 1951. The year 1974 also saw Lynyrd Skynyrd make a bluesy and pointed political statement powered by guitarist Ed King on "Sweet Home Alabama," while that "little ole band from Texas," ZZ Top with the Reverend Billy F. Gibbons, went looking and shuffling for some "Tush" in 1975. In 1976, another band from Boston named after their native city, with lead guitarist Tom Scholz, rejuvenated the waning hard rock years with "Long Time" among other hits on their eponymous debut album. A year later, the British Empire provided Queen and the melodic hard rock chops of Brian May on "We Will Rock You," while UFO sported the fluid "Euro-blues" of German Michael Shenker on "Lights Out," even as the American studio band Ram Jam with guitarist Bill Bartlett significantly updated an obscure Leadbelly song with a controversial and pounding version of "Black Betty." In Los Angeles, a young original hard rock band featuring a new emerging guitar hero named Eddie Van Halen revisited the early sixties with a sledgehammer version of the Kinks' "You Really Got Me" on their debut album in 1978.

Again proving its universality, classic blues rock from Canadian Pat Travers found him "Snortin' Whiskey" and playing blazing blues in Quebec in 1980. Despite the trendy "new wave" rock of the eighties that turned away from the blues and denigrated long, improvised guitar solos, blues-based rockers maintained their dedication to the genre and indeed, many are still rocking hard. As if to confirm the timeless appeal of classic rock to players and listeners alike, Guns N' Roses finally released their long anticipated and "retro" *Chinese Democracy* to great expectations in 2008 after lead singer Axl Rose "legislated" for 14 years.

–Dave Rubin

Acknowledgments

I would like to thank Nick Koukotas for his friendship and help. In addition, Mike Mitchell and Jack Ely of the Kingsmen and Bill Bartlett of Ram Jam were exceptionally gracious and generous with their time.

Dedication

I would like to dedicate this book to my wife Cheryl, daughter Michelle, and friends Ira Bolterman, Darrell Bridges, John Griffith, Bruce Iglauer, Edward Komara, Susie McKay Koval, Eric Leblanc, and Dick Shurman.

About the CD

The accompanying audio CD with this book includes all 25 solos performed note for note with a full band and is playable on any CD player. For PC and MAC computer users, the CD is enhanced with Amazing Slow Downer software so you can adjust the recording to any tempo without changing pitch!

The time code shown at the start of each solo transcription indicates the point at which the solo begins in the original recording.

All music on the CD performed by:
Guitar: Doug Boduch
Bass: Tom McGirr
Keyboards: Warren Wiegatz
Drums: Scott Schroedl

Recorded, mixed, and mastered by Jim Reith at Beathouse Music in Milwaukee, WI, and Jake Johnson at Paradyme Productions in Madison, WI.

Contents

Mike Mitchell

© Getty

> ## "F*ck"
>
> —Drummer Easton, just before verse 2 when he drops a drumstick

Whether considered one of 25 great rock guitar solos or 2,500 classic rock songs, "Louie, Louie" occupies a unique position with over 1,000 cover versions. In the rawest of musical terms, it was the catalyst for everything raucous, rude, and rebellious in the music and youth culture that spawned it.

West Coast R&B singer Richard Berry (1935–1997) wrote and recorded the Calypso-flavored "Louie Louie" in 1957 after being inspired by "El Loco Cha Cha" recorded by Cuban Rene Touzet, as well as Chuck Berry's "Havana Moon" (1956). It remained a regional hit, and Berry went about his career. By 1961, however, the Fabulous Wailers from the Spokane/Tacoma, Washington area, had cut a rock 'n' roll version that became a virtual blueprint for the Kingsmen. In addition, Little Bill and the Blue Notes also waxed poetic with it in 1962.

The Kingsmen were formed in 1957 in Portland, Oregon by Jack Ely (lead vocals and rhythm guitar), Mike Mitchell (lead guitar), Don Galucci (piano), Bob Nordby (bass), and Lynn Easton (drums). They became a popular local attraction playing a variety of R&B and rock covers, including a long instrumental version of "Louie, Louie" in their sets that drove audiences wild. In 1963, Northwest Recorders studio was booked for $36 so the band could record it as a demo to get work on a cruise ship. Ely shouted the words into an overhead mic, slurring his diction of the innocent lyrics, and the myth began.

The cruise line rejected the tape, but it became a radio jingle for the Kingsmen's upcoming appearances. When requests poured in, a few hundred copies were pressed. Paul Revere and the Raiders had also recorded an ad-lib'd version a week after the Kingsmen in the same studio, and the two competed for airplay. Scepter/Wand Records in New York released the Kingsmen single, b/w their original instrumental "Haunted Castle," into several major markets, and it rocked to #2 on *Billboard* and #1 on the *Cashbox* charts. As it started to slip, charges were levied that the lyrics to "Louie, Louie" as sung by Ely were obscene, and the FCC and FBI made absurd investigations as the record was banned in many locales. Consequently, sales rebounded and the record was actually re-released in 1964, 65, and 66.

Meanwhile, a split had occurred in the band when Easton decided he wanted to be a lead singer like Mark Lindsey with Paul Revere. Ely went off and performed with his own version of the Kingsmen and the Courtmen, while Easton and lead

The Kingsmen "check-mated" the other northwest bands with their quintessential version of "Louie, Louie."

guitarist Mitchell, the only original members, led a new unit with Easton lip-syncing "Louie, Louie" whenever possible on shows like "Shindig," "Hullabaloo," and "American Bandstand." Bassist Norm Sundholm left in 1963 to found Sunn Amplifiers as a way to furnish the loud Kingsmen with even more wattage as the Easton-led band scored hits with covers of "Money" (#16) and "Little Latin Lupe Lu" (#46) in 1964 and the original "The Jolly Green Giant" (#4) in 1965. In addition, the band toured incessantly to phenomenal acclaim while setting attendance records.

The following decades found the band, without Ely and then Easton after 1967, rocking on with numerous personnel changes, though Ely headlined the 30th Anniversary Louie Louie Tour in 1993. Also in the nineties, the Kingsmen won a lawsuit against Gusto Records and GML and received back royalties from 1993 on and mechanical rights to their catalog. Meanwhile, Richard Berry, who had sold his rights for $750 in 1959, received $2 million in back royalties in 1986 thanks to the efforts of an artist's rights group.

How to Play It

Though Kingsmen axeman Mike Mitchell clearly used Richard Dangel's solo from the Wailers' version of "Louie, Louie" as a template, the comparison is akin to a match race between a 1963 327 Chevy Super Sport Impala and a 1961 6-banger Nash Rambler. Mitchell hauls butt right off the line and keeps firing on all 8 cylinders through all 16 measures of his rock guitar landmark.

The solo is performed over the same two-measure chord increment of A–D and Em–D that powers the verse and chorus. Observe that the use of Em as the V chord in the key of A, rather than E major or, better yet, E7, is an unusual occurrence in popular music, and it appears in all recordings of "Louie" from Richard Berry on. The result is one of barely submerged malevolence that is perfectly in keeping with the maniacal raving of Jack Ely on the Kingsmen version.

The youthful Mitchell expertly works the root position of the A blues scale at fret 5 while using several musical ideas as motifs. A subtle but significant factor in making the solo so memorable is his regular inclusion of the E♭ (♭5th) "blue note" on string 3 at fret 8 as a motif that is one of the defining characteristics of the blues scale. In measures 2–6, 11, and 12, he combines it with a gliss or pull-off to the 4th (D) at fret 7 that just happens to coincide with the D chord to add structure in a classic modal rock 'n' roll solo. True to the spirit of the modal approach, however, Mitchell continually returns and resolves to the root (A) note (on string 1 at fret 5 or string 4 at fret 7), or for extra musical weight, to the double stop of A/E at fret 5 on strings 1 and 2 as a motif. Check out how he utilizes a selection of hip blues scale notes to produce tart tension preceding resolution that occurs in virtually every measure. Foremost among these are the C (♭3rd) on string 1 at fret 8 that he bends a cool quarter step to the "true blue note" in between the C and C♯ (major 3rd) as seen in measures 1, 5, and 11. Next is that gritty E♭ that shows up in measure 2 on beat 2, and is bent up to from the D note on beat 3 of measure 5.

Mitchell precedes the high point of his solo in measures 9–10 with a dynamic shift in register and phrasing to the open-string position of the A blues scale in measure 8. Employing the open 1st string in conjunction with the E note at fret 5 and the D note at fret 3, he down-shifts on string 2 to fret 1 before ending the measure with the open 1st string. He then pounds the root A note with swinging, syncopated phrasing in what is the simplest but most effective way to focus energy and create musical tension through repetition. Measures 11–12 contain licks similar to the beginning of the solo, while Mitchell returns in measure 14 to the low-register licks from measure 8 as a way to "bookend" his solo before cleverly making the transition back to the verse (not shown) by playing smaller voicings of the chords in measures 15–16.

Vital Stats

Guitarist: Mike Mitchell

Song: "Louie, Louie"

Album: *The Kingsmen in Person* – The Kingsmen

Age at time of recording: 19

Guitar: 1962 Fender Stratocaster

Amp: Pre-CBS Fender Bandmaster

1:26

Guitar Solo
Moderate Rock ♩ = 124

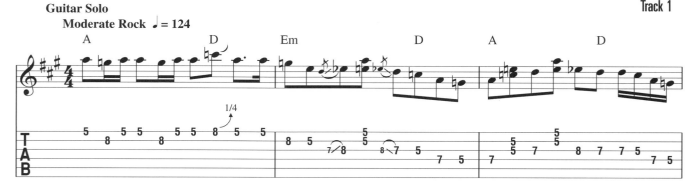

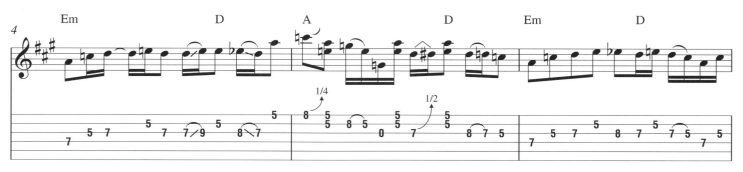

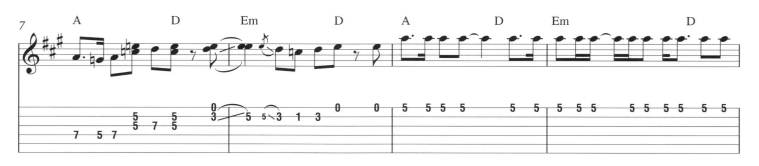

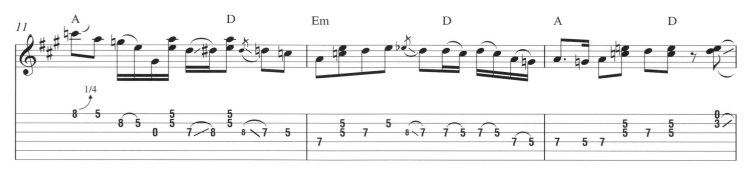

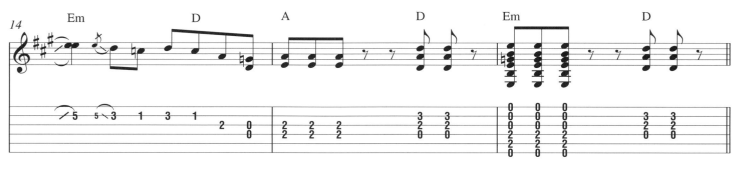

Words and Music by Richard Berry
© 1957 (Renewed 1985) EMI LONGITUDE MUSIC
All Rights Reserved   International Copyright Secured   Used by Permission

Jeff Beck

"In the middle of my solos, I would hear a shhh, shhh sound"

—Jeff Beck describing singer Keith Relf spraying his throat atomizer on stage

The Beatles, Stones, and the Who were bigger, but the "blueswailing" Yardbirds were the hippest band to come out of the British Invasion. Named after the legendary bebop alto saxophonist Charlie "Yardbird" Parker, they provided a launching pad for three of the greatest and most influential guitarists of all time: Eric Clapton, Jeff Beck, and Jimmy Page.

The Metropolis Blues Quartet of the early sixties evolved into the Yardbirds by 1963 with Keith Relf (lead vocals, harmonica), Chris Dreja (rhythm guitar), Paul Samwell-Smith (bass), Jim McCarty (drums), and Anthony "Top" Topham (lead guitar). After a short stint, 16-year-old Topham left and recommended one Eric Patrick Clapton. With young "Slowhand" strutting his vaunted vibrato and phrasing on blues covers like "I Ain't Got You," "I Wish You Would," and the original blues instrumental "Got to Hurry," the band electrified the London R&B scene and followed the Stones into residency at the Crawdaddy Club.

The Yardbirds were just another good R&B band until 1964, however, when they began including "rave ups," or improvisational instrumental jams, into their live sets. *Five Live Yardbirds* shows them at their most frenetic. However, lack of substantial commercial success led to a momentous change of direction when they recorded "For Your Love" in early 1965. It would climb to the top of the charts in the UK and #6 in the U.S. as a pop classic, but the decision did not sit well with "blues purist" Clapton, and he left just as the tune was hitting in March, eventually landing with John Mayall and the Bluesbreakers.

Jimmy Page was tapped to replace Clapton, but demurred in order to continue his lucrative session work. He nominated Jeff Beck, who had also been sounded out by John Mayall and had surreptitiously cut tracks with the Yardbirds, including "For Your Love," "Heart Full of Soul," "Steeled Blues," and "Still I'm Sad" while Clapton was still hanging around grousing. For 18 months, through December of 1966, Beck experienced an explosive creative surge on a rave up version of Bo Diddley's "I'm a Man," "Lost Woman," a landmark cover of "The Train Kept A-Rollin'" (see Aerosmith), "Shapes of Things," and the sitar-like "Over Under Sideways Down" b/w "Jeff's Boogie" among many others. Before he left, however, a "dream team" was formed

Jeff Beck in the Yardbirds turned the concept of rock guitar inside out with his uninhibited rave ups.

when Samwell-Smith departed and Jimmy Page eagerly stepped into his shoes. Dreja hastily switched to bass as the Beck/Page tandem briefly blazed on "Happenings Ten Years Time Ago"/ "Psycho Daisies" and made an appearance with the band in Antonioni's *Blow-Up*, playing "The Train Kept A-Rollin'" recast as "Stroll On."

When Beck split to go solo, Page took the band in a heavier direction, but mismanagement led to their demise in 1968 following *Little Games*. Relf and McCarty formed the folk-rock group Renaissance, while Page briefly led the "New Yardbirds," which evolved into Led Zeppelin. After his stint with the Bluesbreakers, Clapton went on to star in Cream and Blind Faith before launching an ongoing solo career, as did Beck, following a succession of Jeff Beck Groups while turning down the Stones after Mick Taylor quit. In 1976, Keith Relf died tragically when he was electrocuted by his poorly grounded guitar.

In 1984, Dreja, Samwell-Smith, and McCarty convened a Yardbirds reunion named Box of Frogs with guest guitarists including Beck appearing on their self-titled debut album. For their second release in 1986, *Strange Land*, Page lent his estimable presence before they folded. In 2003, Dreja and McCarty formed the New Yardbirds with guitarist Gypie Mayo, releasing an album titled *Birdland* (with guests again including Beck) and touring the U.S.

How to Play It

The extraordinary "El Becko" is second only to Hendrix in the rock guitar pantheon. However, in a rare moment of questionable judgment, he nicked Chuck Berry's obscure instrumental "Guitar Boogie" from 1958 and shamelessly turned it into his "Boogie" without attribution, though "Louie's Guitar Boogie" from 1947 with guitarist Louis Speigner may be the original source. Containing Berry's humorous quote from "Mary Had a Little Lamb" along with his own breathtaking speed and raunchy blues bends, to name just a few of the tricks up his fringed sleeve, Beck recreates a bluesy, jazzy instrumental conjured from ten 12-bar blues progressions given rehearsal letters A–J.

Each 12-bar section contains a different form of unaccompanied improvisation in measures 1–4 followed by measures 5–12 with similar chord comping throughout with the band and subtle overdubbed parts all played by the "Beckster." Rehearsal Letters A, B, and C provide a select overview of the various approaches presented in the tune. In letter A, Beck (Gtr. 1) mimics Berry with a swing-type intro reminiscent of "Johnny B. Goode" and "Roll Over, Beethoven" that bangs on the root G note of the G5 chord change in measures 1–3 for musical tension through repetition before running down the *G composite blues scale* (blues scale plus Mixolydian mode) in root position with slithery pull-offs to open strings 1, 2, 3, and 4.

In letter B, Beck (Gtrs. 1 & 2) again pays "homage" to the "Father of Rock 'n' Roll" by quoting the melody to the first line of "Mary Had a Little Lamb" (or "London Bridge Is Falling Down") with harmonies in 3rds, just like Berry did in his fifth chorus. Observe that the melody appears on string 2 with the harmony above it on string 1 (doubled by Gtr. 3 on string 3 in measures 13–16) in a manner often favored by Berry and that may have been acquired from Western Swing music. Duane Allman and Dickey Betts as a tandem perfected the technique to high art in the early Allman Brothers Band.

Beck breaks loose in letter C with aggressive blues licks derived from the composite blues scale at the sixth and eighth positions that still have the power to delight over 40 years later. Check out the classic "Albert King bend" of C to D that resolves to the root G on string 2 in measure 25. Also observe how Beck plays linearly on string 1 in a vocal-like manner via the melodic half steps between C and B and the chromatic licks of B♭, B, and C in measures 26 and 27. Note that it is totally in keeping with the uniquely expressive style of a man not known for his singing prowess!

Vital Stats

Guitarist: Jeff Beck

Song: "Jeff's Boogie"

Album: *Over Under Sideways Down* – The Yardbirds

Age at time of recording: 22

Guitar: 1956 Fender Esquire

Amp: Vox AC30

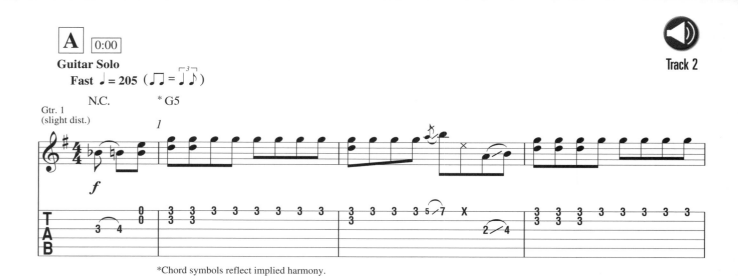

*Chord symbols reflect implied harmony.

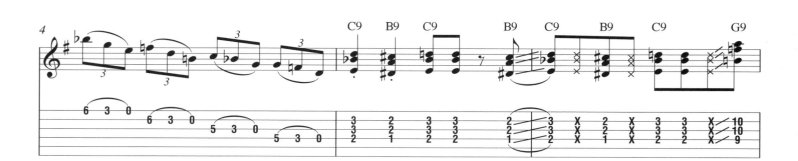

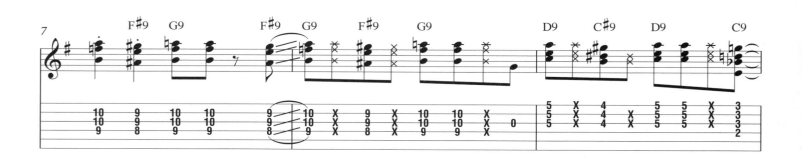

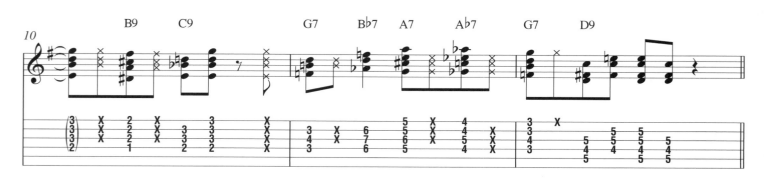

Words and Music by Jeff Beck
© 1966 (Renewed 1994) B. FELDMAN & CO., LTD. trading as YARDBIRDS MUSIC CO.
All Rights for the U.S. and Canada Controlled and Administered by GLENWOOD MUSIC CORP.
All Rights Reserved   International Copyright Secured   Used by Permission

Eric Clapton

Eric Clapton had already distinguished himself as a formidable guitar hero in England with the Yardbirds and with John Mayall and the Bluesbreakers when he formed Cream. The pioneering, pyrotechnical power trio and "supergroup" would reach their zenith with *Wheels of Fire* but unfortunately crash and burn out shortly thereafter.

In 1966 at a London gig, drummer Ginger Baker sat in with the Bluesbreakers who had recently hired bassist/singer/harmonicist Jack Bruce. Clapton, who was already being hailed by his idolatrous fans for his groundbreaking blues solos, saw the opportunity to stretch far beyond the confines of traditional 12-bar blues. He formed Cream with Bruce and Baker with the name immodestly implying that they were the "cream" of guitarists, bassists, and drummers. The rhythm section had previously played in the R&B Graham Bond Organisation, while Bruce had also briefly been with Manfred Mann, and they frequently fought bitterly, including throughout Cream. Their debut *Fresh Cream* (#39) in late 1966, though shaky in its original material, was influential far beyond its chart position and sales as it blew down the door for rock guitar virtuosity and the incorporation of powerful classic blues licks into rock and pop. In addition, it introduced rock to the obligatory drum solo courtesy of the overwhelming double bass drum theatrics of Baker.

The cleverly named *Disraeli Gears* (#4) a year later with producer Felix Pappalardi consolidated their heavy blues and psychedelic-rock tendencies to produce landmark classics like "Sunshine of Your Love" (#5), the Albert King tribute "Strange Brew," and the surrealistic "Tales of Brave Ulysses" that foreshadowed "White Room" to come. The titanic double-disc *Wheels of Fire* (#1 and #11 Black Albums!) in 1968, divided into live tracks like the breathtaking "Crossroads" (#28) and studio tracks highlighted by "White Room" (#6), shows the growing improvisational majesty of Clapton, the innovative and imaginative songwriting of Bruce, and the locomotive drums of Baker. It also, unfortunately, displays the three massive egos colliding, which would quickly "derail" the thundering express in November of 1968. The posthumous *Goodbye* (#2) in 1969 ended Cream's meteoric rise with a bang and a format similar to the previous album. "Badge" (#60), co-written by George Harrison under a nom de plume, is an acknowledged classic, while the live side with Skip James's "I'm So Glad," "Politician," and "Sitting on Top of the World" glows with improvisational brilliance.

Clapton almost immediately jumped to the ill-fated "supergroup" Blind Faith, featuring Steve Winwood, with Baker in tow. A stint with Delaney & Bonnie & Friends preceded his going solo,

"*Clapton is God.*"
——Graffiti in London during the Bluesbreakers era

A black light made the psychedelic album cover glow while Clapton burned like a blues laser in the grooves.

9

highlighted by his short-lived band Derek and the Dominos featuring Duane Allman. When Allman returned to the Brothers, Neal Schon was briefly tapped to fill the position before the Dominos folded. Since then, Clapton has maintained a productive, if uneven, solo career. Baker was involved in a number of inconsequential projects, while Bruce began a solo career and then played in a number of power blues rock groups with Leslie West and Robin Trower. In 1993, Cream was inducted into the Rock and Roll Hall of Fame.

Clapton was inducted into the Rock and Roll Hall of Fame in 2000 for his solo career and, along with his previous induction with the Yardbirds in 1992, makes him the only triple honoree to date. In 2005, Cream reunited with an obviously reluctant Clapton and played a series of successful gigs in London, ending with three artistically disappointing dates at Madison Square Garden in New York. In 2006, the band was honored with a Lifetime Achievement Award at the Grammys.

How to Play It

His buddy and alter ego Jimi Hendrix preceded him in use of the wah-wah pedal, but Eric Clapton immortalized the ubiquitous sixties psychedelic effect forever on "White Room." His basic approach of rhythmically rocking back and forth on the pedal in time to the music would become the blueprint for a generation of guitarists, though few had his fire or blues credibility.

Clapton runs amok over the two-measure descending and dramatic vamp of D5–Csus2 and G/B–B♭5–C5 from the verse (not shown) in the D minor pentatonic scale. Remaining mostly in the root position with brief forays into the extension position, he manages to maintain rolling expanses of musical tension for over 26 measures with unbridled aggressive riffing. Playing modally, he builds momentum to a satisfying climax by composing his solo in fluidly connected sections of 2, 3, 4, and 6 measures in length. Measures 1–6 include the blues-approved bend of the 4th (G) to the 5th (A) on string 3 at fret 12 that functions as a motif and the signature sound of the solo. Observe how Clapton "inverts" the classic opening blues lick in measures 1 and 2 by following the D and C notes on beat 2 with a repeat of the bend on beat 3 as a way to boost the forward motion. Measures 7–8 quickly jack up the energy with fleet, repeating quadruplets in the extension position of the D minor pentatonic scale, while measures 9–12 revert back to the tight cluster of notes mainly on strings 4, 3, and 2 in the root position. First shown in measures 4–6, they offer a sense of resolution due to repetition on the root D note. A leap up to the extension position in measures 12 and 13 offers a short but dynamic change in register.

Clapton returns to his main theme in the root position in measures 14–17, introduced by a dynamically soaring bend of one-and-a-half steps of A (5th) to C (♭7th). The measures are sparked again by the bend of G to A in order to tightly focus the energy as preparation for what follows. In measures 18 and 19, he proffers an even more dynamic change when he inserts vibrant harmony into the action with C/A double stops and singing bends of one-and-a-half steps in the extension position from D to the nasty F (♭3rd) "blues note." After yet another return to the root position in measure 20 for resolution to the D notes and as a "buffer," Clapton expands the scale in measures 21–22 to include the root note on string 1 at fret 10 while also reintroducing pointed bends as a precursor to the climactic measures preceding the fade out. Measure 23, as a respite, is similar to measure 20 as a way to intensify the power of measures 24–26, which feature the startling series of G to A bends on string 3 and A to B bends on string 2. Combined with his vigorous rocking of the wah pedal, Clapton creates a rubbery sensation that is as surrealistic as Pete Brown's lyrics as vocalized by Jack Bruce.

Vital Stats

Guitarist: Eric Clapton

Song: "White Room"

Album: *Wheels of Fire* – Cream

Age at time of recording: 23

Guitar: 1963 Gibson ES-335

Amp: Marshall 50 watt head with 4x12 cabinet

Outro-Guitar Solo
Moderate Rock ♩ = 116

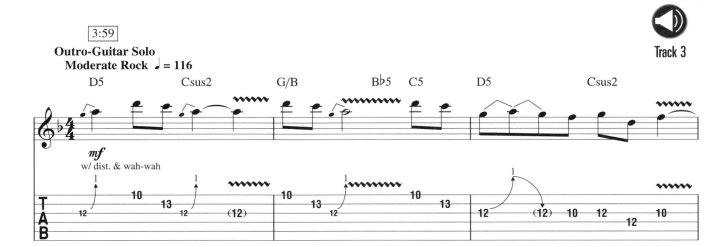

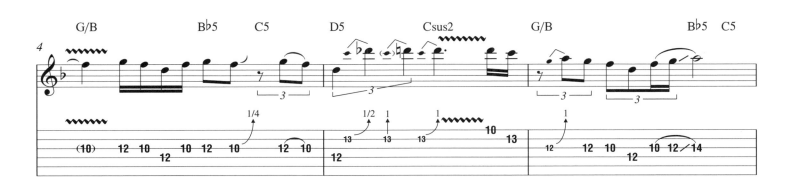

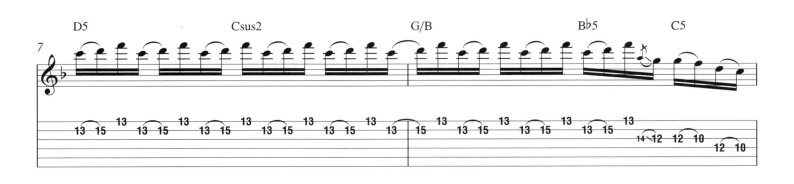

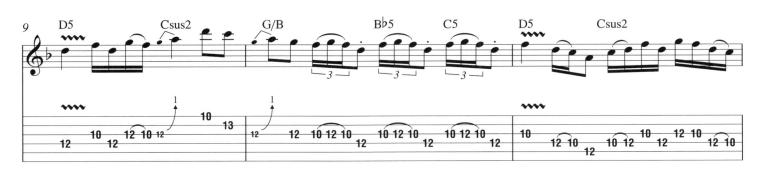

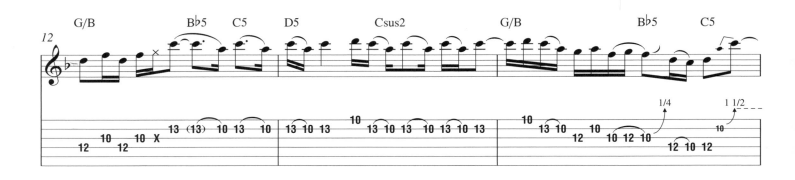

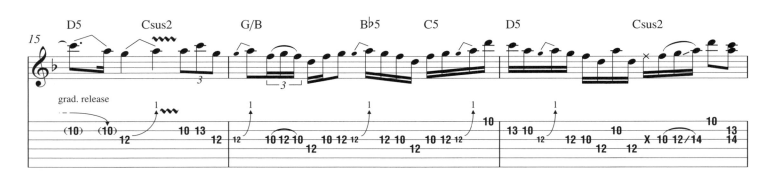

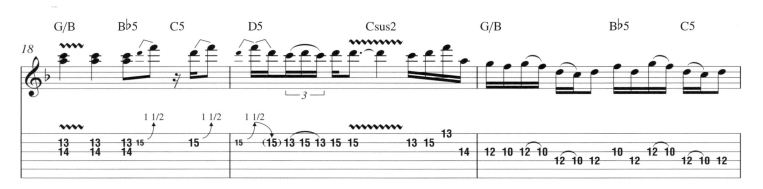

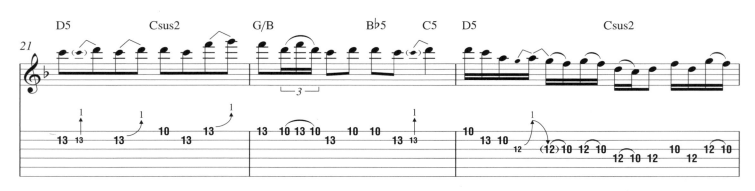

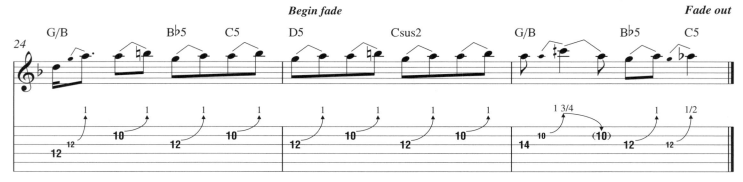

John Fogerty

"We were the #7 act on the bill, bottom of the totem pole. And as the first guys to go on, we were the last to sound check before they opened the doors. It was like, 'Here's the drums, boom, boom; here's the guitar, clank, clank.' I looked over at the guys and said, 'Hey, follow this!' Basically, it was the riff and the attitude of 'Born on the Bayou,' without the words."

—John Fogerty describing how he wrote the song at the Avalon Ballroom in San Francisco in 1968

© Photofest

When "Proud Mary" b/w "Born on the Bayou" was on the charts, Creedence Clearwater Revival had never even been South. Nonetheless, leader John Fogerty evoked plenty of rural America through the pitch-perfect craft of his songwriting. John Cameron Fogerty was born on May 28, 1945, in El Cerrito, California. Though James Burton was his guitar "god," it was Duane Eddy's hooky bass riffs that he tried to emulate in his writing. His mother encouraged him and his brother Tom to pursue their interest in music, and by 1958, Tom was playing guitar in the Playboys while John and his friends, Stu Cook on bass and Doug Clifford on drums, were performing as the instrumental trio the Blue Velvets. Eventually, Tom came in and took over, renaming the group Tommy Fogerty and the Blue Velvets.

In 1963, Fantasy Records offered a contract if they changed their name to the Golliwogs, but in 1966, owner Saul Zaentz suggested another change. "Creedence" was the name of Tom's friend, "Clearwater" was from a beer commercial, and "Revival" referred to the revitalization of the band. The epochal *Creedence Clearwater Revival*, in 1968, promptly went gold at #58 on the charts. *Bayou Country* (1969) established John as one of the finest tunesmiths around at #7 on the pop charts and #41 on the black albums chart (!), featuring the gold single "Proud Mary" (#2) b/w "Born on the Bayou." Continuing, the combo saw their second gold single, "Bad Moon Rising" (#2) b/w "Lodi," and a third gold single, "Green River" (#2) b/w "Commotion," released before they came out on the #1 platinum album *Green River*. They appeared at Woodstock, though John foolishly refused to have their performance included in the famed movie and soundtrack. Their fourth gold single, "Down on the Corner" (#3) b/w "Fortunate Son," was followed by their third platinum album, the #3 pop (#28 black album) *Willy and the Poor Boys*.

The kinetic cover photo only hinted at the time-less, classic roots rock John Fogerty had crafted with every track.

In 1970, "Travelin' Band" b/w "Who'll Stop the Rain" was their fifth gold single at #2. "Up Around the Bend" b/w "Run Through the Jungle" was the sixth gold single at #4 and *Cosmo's Factory* promptly became their fourth platinum platter at #1, containing "Lookin' out My Back Door" b/w "Long as I Can See the Light" at #2 as their seventh gold disc. Resentment by Tom and the others for John's autocratic running of Creedence was coming to a boil despite their success via his efforts. Nonetheless, the year ended with *Pendulum* garnering one million advance orders, guaranteeing a fifth platinum award even before it peaked at #5 with "Have You Ever Seen the Rain" b/w "Hey Tonight" (#8), their eighth gold single. Tom quit the band to pursue a solo career as their ninth Top 10 single "Sweet Hitch-Hiker" (#6) b/w "Door to Door" was released, followed by their last single, "Someday Never Comes" b/w "Tearin' Up the Country." The last CCR studio album, *Mardi Gras*, was released in 1972 to critical panning and marked an inglorious end to one of the greatest rock 'n' roll bands.

The years since have been a mixed bag for John, tragic for brother Tom, and pathetic for Cook and Clifford. John launched his solo career in 1972, but the next year he began disastrous legal actions against Saul Zaentz and Fantasy Records. Tom died at the age of 48 in 1990 from AIDs after contracting the disease through a blood transfusion. When CCR was inducted into the Rock and Roll Hall of Fame in 1993, John refused to jam with Cook and Clifford who went on to form Creedence Clearwater Revisited in 1995. From his #1 charting "comeback" album *Centerfield* in 1985 to *Deja Vu (All Over Again)* (#23) in 2004, John has managed to make music that still presents his vision of classic American rock 'n' roll.

How to Play It

John Fogerty was known to tune his guitar down a whole step on many songs, such as "Proud Mary" and "Bad Moon Rising." But for "Born on the Bayou," he is in standard tuning and provides a tutorial on how to be creative in the key of E. Fogerty acknowledges a major debt to the blues, though he is not a single-note improviser in the B.B. King mode, for example. Instead, he composes his best solos by combining riffs and licks in logical sequences that always lead to a big "payoff" and conclusion.

The 21-measure solo (not counting the repeats) of "Born on the Bayou" consists of four discrete, distinctive sections that follow each other like an "old hound dog chasin' down a hoo-doo." Measures 1–8, for all intents and purposes, utilize the E, G♯, A, B, and D notes in the open position of the E Mixolydian mode, reflecting the E7 chord as played by rhythm guitarist Tom Fogerty (not shown). Like almost all solos in popular music, and especially the modal variety based around one chord change, the strategy is to alternate passages of musical tension and anticipation with resolution. Hence, Fogerty repeats a pull-off from the A to the G♯ note in measures 2, 3, 4, 6, and 7 as a motif that builds a degree of anticipation and resolves to the root note E in measures 3, 4, 7, and 8. Observe the arpeggios implying E7 in measures 5 and 6 which also provide brief resolution, as well as dynamics by virtue of the higher register involved.

Measures 9–14 contain double stops in 6ths derived from the E Mixolydian mode that provide sumptuous chord melody against the E7 vamp of the rhythm, as well as forward motion that builds power to the next section. Be aware that the six measures are constructed from two-measure increments. Measures 9, 11, and 13 are nearly identical and function as the "call" while measures 10, 12, and 14 serve as the "response." Notice that measure 14, however, does not resolve the musical tension, but instead uses anticipation to point the way directly to measures 15–18 of the third section.

Using triads for the D, A, and E chords and descending 6ths from the E Mixolydian mode, Fogerty creates a two-measure phrase repeated three times that resolves firmly in each measure. Along with measure 17 of the D, A, and E changes and measure 18 where the E chord sustains, it is the climactic release of the solo. Measures 19–22 contain a two-measure bass-string riff that repeats three times and functions as a bridge back to the intro pattern. Derived from the E major pentatonic scale at the second position, it provides the perfect "bookend" to the solo while smoothly setting up the transition and entry back to the signature E7 riff.

Vital Stats

Guitarist: John Fogerty

Song: "Born on the Bayou"

Album: *Bayou Country –* Creedence Clearwater Revival

Age at time of recording: 24

Guitar: 1969 Rickenbacker 325 Fireglo

Amp: 1968 Kustom K200A-4

Words and Music by John Fogerty
Copyright © 1968 Jondora Music
Copyright Renewed
International Copyright Secured   All Rights Reserved

Paul McCartney, George Harrison, John Lennon

© Photofest

The Rolling Stones may be the "World's Greatest Rock 'n' Roll Band," but the Beatles were the greatest songwriters and arguably the most influential pop musicians of the twentieth century. The cultural earthquake they created was without precedent and will likely never be repeated.

The Beatles' story virtually begins and ends with John Lennon. He started playing guitar in the Quarrymen in

> ## "We don't like their sound, and guitar music is on the way out."
> —Decca Recording Company rejecting the Beatles in 1962

Liverpool in the mid-fifties and added guitarist Paul McCartney in 1957, followed by guitarist George Harrison. They became the Silver Beatles in 1960 and then just the Beatles, in honor of Buddy Holly's Crickets, with Lennon making wordplay by spelling it with an "A." Stu Sutcliffe (bass) and Pete Best (drums) completed the quintet just before they went to Hamburg, Germany, for marathon gigs that whipped them into fighting trim. Further evolution took place when they returned to play legendary performances at the birthplace of the "Merseybeat" sound: the Cavern Club in Liverpool.

In 1961, they returned to Hamburg, though Sutcliffe would quit and tragically die in 1962. McCartney reluctantly took over on bass, and the quartet made their first recordings

backing Tony Sheridan. By the end of the year, the Beatles' burgeoning popularity back home attracted record store owner Brian Epstein, who soon became their manager. After several labels turned them down, producer George Martin at EMI signed them in 1962 as Epstein changed their appearance from rockers to mods. In what has persisted as a controversial move, Pete Best was fired in the summer and replaced by Richard "Ringo Starr" Starkey. Their first single re-cut in the fall, however—"Love Me Do" b/w "P.S. I Love You"—features session drummer Andy White. It made the British Top 20, though it was "Please Please Me" (#2) in early 1963 followed by "From Me to You" (#1) that broke the band commercially. Their debut LP, *Please Please Me*, held the #1 spot for 30 weeks and in combination with TV appearances, "Beatlemania" stormed the British Isles.

"I Want to Hold Your Hand" (#1) was the first single released in the U.S. on December 26, 1963, and their appearances on the "Ed Sullivan Show" in early 1964 were both historic and hysterical. Their timing was fortuitous, along with every other aspect of the band. After the assassination of JFK in

Though walking in a line, the Beatles were determined to go their separate ways after Abbey Road, and McCartney was barefoot only because it was hot, not because he was "dead."

November 1963, their exuberance and "innocence" was the perfect tonic for a mourning nation and not only signaled the start of Beatlemania beyond Great Britain and the subsequent musical "British Invasion," but also the official start of the counterculture sixties.

After a concert at Candlestick Park in San Francisco in 1966, the Beatles never performed live again before paying fans, as the non-stop screaming made it impossible for them to hear properly. Instead, they concentrated solely on recordings and would chart 21 singles and 20 albums at #1 while creating innovative recordings every step of the way. Following their ignomious breakup in 1970, all four members would go their own ways with varying degrees of success. McCartney continues to record and perform and has had an extensive career separate from his Beatles legacy. Lennon had innumerable loyal fans until his shocking murder on December 8, 1980, which effectively curtailed endless hope about them getting "back together." Harrison also enjoyed much success as a solo artist and as a member of the Traveling Wilburys until his death on

November 29, 2001. Ringo has had a more modest career, but nonetheless remains active, and his son Zack now plays drums with the Who. McCartney's circumspect answers imply that it is unlikely he and Ringo will ever record together again, though they appeared together at Radio City Music Hall in Manhattan during the spring of 2009 for a benefit concert.

How to Play It

John Lennon liked to say that Eric Clapton thought him a good guitar player, and Paul McCartney had already played great solos on several Beatles recordings, including "Ticket to Ride" and "Taxman." Hence, it was not a stretch when they joined their brilliant lead guitarist George Harrison for a round-robin at "The End" on the occasion of the last Beatles album, making it a cause for bittersweet celebration.

Over 20 measures of an A7–D7 vamp, McCartney, Harrison, and Lennon trade short solos three times. McCartney (Gtr. 1) "leads" off in measures 1 and 2 by choosing the root position of the A minor pentatonic scale to make a bluesy statement. The A/E double stop on beat 1 confirms the A tonality of the key while ending on the G note as the ♭7th in measure 2, which provides musical tension and anticipation to the next solo. Harrison (Gtr. 2) plays in the same scale position through measures 3 and 4 and sounds suspiciously like his close friend Eric Clapton with a slinky bend and vibrato of the C bent to D on string 1 at fret 8 in measure 3. Lennon (Gtr. 3), by comparison, goes his own way with blasting triads at fret 12 implying A9 and G in measure 5 and C (or Am) in measure 6 with E/C at fret 5.

For the second round, McCartney cleverly sneaks in the hip D♯ note as the ♭5th blues note on string 3 at fret 8 in measure 7. However, he does finish on the root D note for resolution in measure 8, adding vibrato to the sustained note. Harrison changes course by repeatedly bending the bluesy and dissonant double stops of E/C combined with the root A note in measure 9 and then following suit with the double stop of F♯/D that implies the D chord in measure 10 over D7. In dynamic opposition, Lennon roars on the bass strings in measures 11 and 12. Observe that, in measure 11, he bends the B note on string 5 at fret 2 from the Mixolydian mode one step to the major tonality-defining C♯, and a half step to C—a prominent note of tension in the blues scale. In measure 12, he acknowledges "old tyme" country blues by bending the C a quarter step to one of the "true blue notes" in between C (♭3rd) and C♯ (major 3rd).

In the last round, the "cute Beatle" turns the wick up with taut repetition on the G and C notes for peak tension in measure 13 before zipping down in measure 14 to the open position recently vacated by Lennon. Check out how he, too, cannot resist the funky quarter-step bend on the C note at fret 3, followed by the C♯ at fret 4, and then quick resolution to the open 5th string. The "quiet Beatle," meanwhile, flies to the opposite end of the fingerboard in the twelfth position of the A minor pentatonic scale highlighted by a soaring bend from G to A across the bar line between measures 15 and 16. In addition, not wanting to be trumped by his mates in the blues shootout, he bends the C to the "true blue note" on string 2 at fret 13. Leaving it to Lennon to take it home, the "smart Beatle" wisely decides to make a big musical climax with alternating thundering triads of F♯/D/A pulled off to E/C/G before conclusively ending on a cool A7 triple stop on beat 1 of measure 19.

Vital Stats

Guitarist: Paul McCartney, George Harrison, John Lennon

Song: "The End"

Album: *Abbey Road –* The Beatles

Age at time of recording: 27, 26, and 29, respectively

Guitar: 1962 Epiphone Casino (McCartney), 1957 refinished Les Paul Standard "Lucy" (Harrison), 1966 Epiphone Casino (Lennon)

Amp: CBS Silverface Fender Twin Reverbs

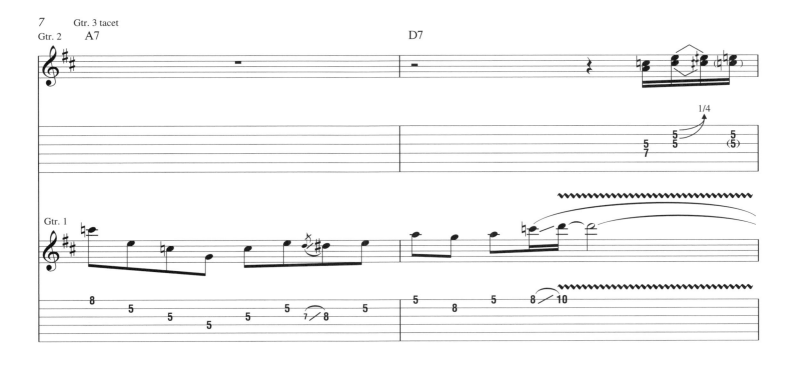

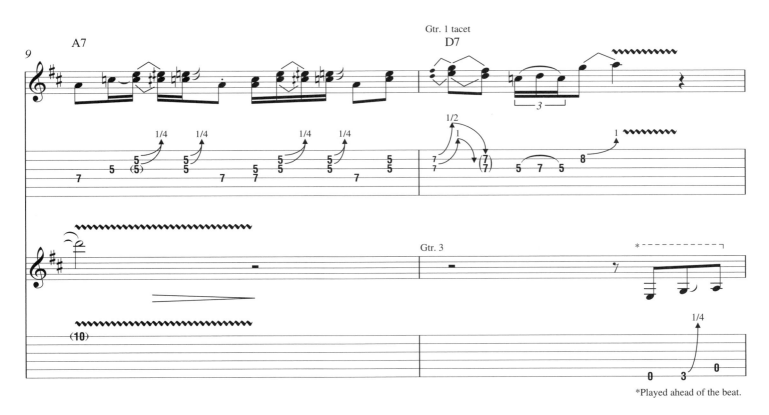

*Played ahead of the beat.

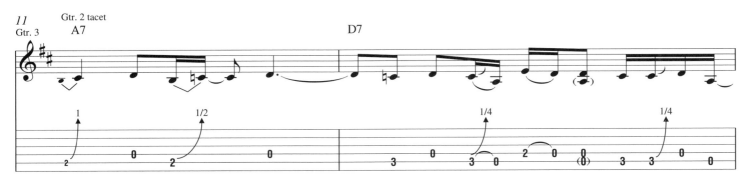

Carlos Santana

Carlos Santana confounded every popular stereotype in the late sixties as a Mexican who merged exuberant, syncopated Latin rhythms with rock, blues, and jazz to produce a new category of music. Still active, winning awards and accolades 40 years later, his virtuosity, creativity, and spirituality propel him ever forward.

Born July 20, 1947, in Jalisco, Mexico, Carlos Augusto Santana Alves began playing the violin at the age of five like his Mariarchi father. He came to the guitar around eight through the blues of B.B. King and John Lee Hooker and began playing in clubs in his teens when the family moved to Tijuana. He moved to San Francisco in the early sixties and formed the Santana Blues Band in 1966. They debuted in 1968 on *The Live Adventures of Michael Bloomfield and Al Kooper* and were signed to Columbia Records as Santana. With Greg Rolie (vocals and keyboards), David Brown

The ferocious lion's head is actually constructed from multicultural human images, making for an apt visual representation of the creative music inside.

(bass), Michael Shrieve (drums), José "Chepito" Areas (percussion), and Michael Carabello (percussion), they toured the U.S. and appeared memorably at Woodstock in August of 1969 just prior to the release of their self-titled debut album (#4), containing "Evil Ways" (#9) and "Soul Sacrifice."

The epochal *Abraxas* followed at #1 in 1970 with Fleetwood Mac's "Black Magic Woman" (#4), Tito Puente's "Oye Como Va" (#20), and the original "Samba Pa Ti." Most significantly, extended instrumental passages boldly revealed Santana's evolving guitar skills and progressive musical direction. By the end of the year, 17-year-old blues guitar wiz Neal Schon was added to the lineup, and the equally spectacular *Santana III* earned another #1 and over two million in sales in 1971. Featuring "Everybody's Everything" (#12) and "No One to Depend On" (#36), it marked the end of the original Santana lineup, with Schon and Rolie eventually forming Journey and Carlos retaining rights to the band name. He would henceforth record and perform with various sidemen, including several original members.

The remainder of the seventies saw Santana become a follower of guru Sri Chinmoy and adopting the name

© Photofest

"Devadip" (the lamp, light, and eye of God). He released respectfully charting albums with his band, highlighted by the gold *Amigos* (#10) in 1976, while also delving into jazz and fusion collaborations with fellow Chinmoy acolyte John McLaughlin, Alice

"Shit, man. That little thing really boogies!"

—Carlos Santana (upon playing a prototype of the Mesa Boogie amp)

Coltrane, and Herbie Hancock. In 1979, he put out his first "solo" album, *Oneness: Silver Dreams – Golden Reality*. The follow up, *Zebop!* in 1981 (#9), sold one million with "Winning" (#17) and a more commercial rock sound. In 1986, he convened a twentieth anniversary reunion concert with former members and in 1987 won his first Grammy for Best Rock Instrumental Performance for the title track of his solo release, *Blues for Salvador*.

A period of decline followed, including *Santana Brothers* in 1994 with Jorge Santana. Santana and his original band were inducted into the Rock and Roll Hall of Fame in 1998 preceding his sensational comeback, *Supernatural* (#1) in 1999, containing "Smooth" (#1) and "Maria" (#1). A guest-laden affair with artists from Eric Clapton to Lauryn Hill and Dave Matthews that minimized his guitar presence, it nonetheless sold 10 million copies and won eight Grammys including Record of the Year for "Smooth" (featuring singer Rob Thomas) and Album of the Year. *Shaman* (#1) in 2002, which won a Grammy for "The Game of Love" (#5) and "Why Don't You and I" (#8), followed the same successful template, as did *All That I Am* (#2) in 2005. In 2006, he toured Europe with his son Salvador as the opening act.

How to Play It

Though his style would progress towards virtuosity as he acquired more chops and scale knowledge via his interest in jazz,

Carlos Santana possessed a unique, signature style from the beginning. Passionate to a fault from the hot Latin music that is his heritage, it is stunning in its syncopation and dynamics.

His first guitar solo after the intro is a classic modal excursion in the A *Dorian* mode, the second mode of the major scale, which is typically played over minor 7 chords. Measures 1–14 vamp on the Am7–D–Am7 chords, while measures 15–22 alternate with Am7 and Bm7 changes and measures 23–26 ride out on Am7. These i–IV (Am–D) changes occur in many genres of popular music, including blues and jazz, as they produce great forward motion. Understand that Bm7 can be a substitute for D, so in essence Am7 and Bm7 are essentially the same harmonic sequence.

Santana locks into the hypnotic and repetitive minor key voicing in measures 1–14 with short, pointed phrases, mostly in the root position of the scale. Notice how he tends to rest on beats 1 and 2 of most measures, using the dramatic "musical space" to intensify the sharp retorts that follow. He establishes the flavor of his scale right off in measure 1 by landing on the F♯ (6th) note that is the defining difference between the Dorian and *Aeolian* (natural minor) modes. With clarity and precision, Santana then plays licks that alternately end by creating anticipation with the C (♭3rd) or resolution to the A (root) notes. Check out how he also alternates between accessing the A note on string 4 string 1, and the C note on string 3 and string 1. Along with the selection of pull-offs that he utilizes, it contributes to a variety of phrasing so necessary in a solo with relatively narrow parameters of scale and note choice. Be sure to see the wide

interval pull-off from the E note at fret 12 to the C note at fret 8 on string 1 in measures 10–11 for a dynamic change of register.

When the progression shifts into the Am7–Bm7 vamp starting in measure 15, Santana glides up and out of the root position of the A Dorian mode with glisses and hammer-ons that deposit him on string 1 above fret 12 into the sweet range of his axe. What follows is a timely lesson in how to be inventive rhythmically as well as melodically in order to rivet the listener's attention. In measures 17–18, he continually repeats the A, E, and F♯ notes on string 1 at frets 17, 12, and 14 in syncopated groupings of three notes to increase the energy. In measures 19–20, he accelerates up to a steady sixteenth-note rhythm with A and F♯, pumping up the musical tension to a phenomenal degree, as do the E and A notes in measures 21–22 where the A note functions as the root of Am7 for resolution and the ♭7th note of Bm7 for anticipation. Having reached the celestial climax of his solo in a flurry of percussive notes, Santana "returns to earth" by rhythmically strumming Am7 voicings in measures 23–24.

Vital Stats

Guitarist: Carlos Santana

Song: "Soul Sacrifice"

Album: *Santana*

Age at time of recording: 22

Guitar: Gibson SG Special w/ P-90 pickups

Amp: Fender Twin Reverb

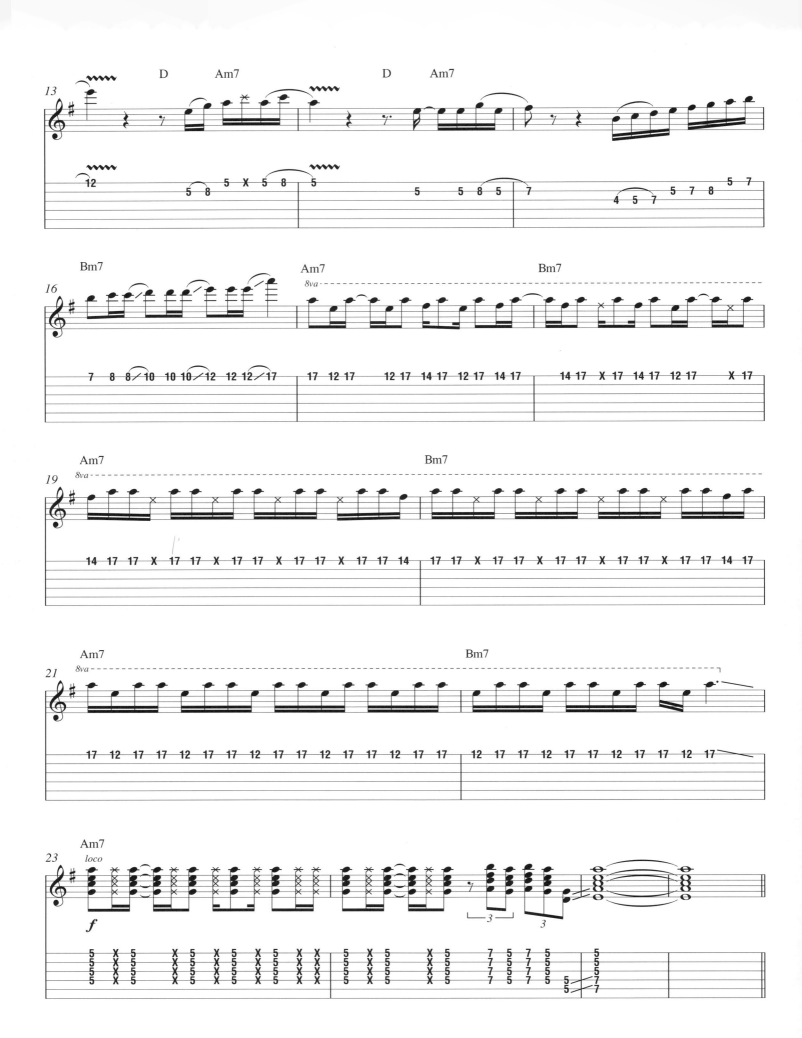

Jimmy Page

British guitarists have had a special affinity for over-amped electric blues since the sixties. John Mayall and the Bluesbreakers were true to Chicago blues, but Led Zeppelin with Jimmy Page exploded the boundaries into thrashing blues rock leavened dynamically with acoustic music.

In 1968, during the slow demise of the Yardbirds, Page fantasized about a supergroup with Jeff Beck and bassist John Entwistle and drummer Keith Moon from the Who—who quipped it would go over like a "lead zeppelin." While playing on Donovan's "Hurdy Gurdy Man," however, he met arranger/bassist/keyboardist John Paul Jones. When 'birds Keith Relf, Jim McCarty, and Chris Dreja left, Page recruited Jones, singer Robert Plant, and drummer John Bonham to go out as the "New Yardbirds" in September; in October, they morphed into Led Zeppelin.

The retouched photo of the German Jasta division that bombed England from zeppelins in WWI, including a head shot of legendary bluesman Blind Willie Johnson, is an appropriate image for the devastating blues rock blasting from Page's axe.

Their epochal debut *Led Zeppelin* (#10) was recorded quickly in early 1969, followed by their first triumphant U.S. tour. *Led Zeppelin II* was a step forward and knocked the Beatles' *Abbey Road* out of the #1 spot (#32 on the Black Albums chart!). *Led Zeppelin III* (#1 and #30 on the Black Albums chart!) had a pronounced British folk bent, and their first single, "The Immigrant Song" (#16), was released against their wishes, as they wanted their albums to be viewed as complete entities. The mighty Zep then released the monumental *Led Zeppelin IV* (#2) in late 1971. It magnificently summed up both their uncompromising blues rock mastery with "Black Dog" (#15) and their mystic folk leanings with "The Battle of Evermore." The crowning achievement was "Stairway to Heaven," which perennially tops reader's polls as the greatest rock song of all time.

Houses of the Holy (#1) in 1973 with "D'yer Mak'er" (#20) and "Over the Hills and Far Away" (#51) contained diverse, original music that avoided the primal blues riffs of old. Two years later, the two-disc *Physical Graffiti* (#1) with "Trampled Underfoot" (#38) was their "White Album" in its broad scope. Unfortunately, Plant and his wife suffered a car accident in Greece that prematurely ended the resulting U.S.

© Photofest

tour. *Presence* (#1) in 1976 did a "turnaround" back to long, epic, blues-based rock that may have hinted at a lull in the creativity of Plant and Page, as did the release of the live *The Song Remains*

"My fingerpicking is sort of a cross between Pete Seeger, Earl Scruggs, and total incompetence..."
—Jimmy Page

the Same (#2) in the fall. Personally worse, Plant lost his six-year-old son Karac to an infection, resulting in a nearly two-year band hiatus.

In the summer of 1979, Led Zeppelin played two shows in Knebworth, which would be their last English concerts, as *In Through the Out Door* (#1), featuring "Fool in the Rain" (#21), was released in the fall. Following a European tour in the spring of 1980, the band was rehearsing for an upcoming U.S. tour when John Bonham died on September 25 after an epic alcoholic binge. In December, they decided to call it quits.

Page, Plant, and Jones all went on with solo careers and side projects, and Zeppelin was inducted into the Rock and Roll Hall of Fame in 1995. Page and Plant played in the Honeydrippers (1984) and reunited for *No Quarter* (1994) and *Walking into Clarksdale* (1998). Led Zeppelin reunions occurred at *Live Aid* (1985), the Atlantic Records 40th Anniversary concert (1988), and for a London concert (2007) with Jason Bonham that received 20 million requests for tickets. Plant recorded and toured with Alison Krauss in 2008, winning five Grammys for their collaboration *Raising Sand*, and has unequivocally declared he is through being a Zeppelin.

How to Play It

Jimmy Page and Robert Plant bridged Robert Johnson and his "Traveling Riverside Blues" to Howlin' Wolf and paid the price for the latter connection. Lyrically and musically, there are sections of "The Lemon Song" that infringe on Wolf's "Killing Floor" from 1965. In 1972, Arc Music, owner of the publishing for Wolf's songs, sued Zeppelin for copyright infringement. An out-of-court settlement eventually resulted in a payout to Wolf and credit on certain albums. Apparently, the original British release listed the song as "Killing Floor" on the label with a credit to Chester Burnett, Wolf's given name. Nonetheless, "Pagey" plays spectacularly throughout.

The 36-measure solo gives him the opportunity to stretch-out luxuriously and with gusto over three 12-bar blues progressions. Taken at a tempo almost double that of the verses (not shown), it is a virtual textbook of choice blues guitar licks. Measures 1–12 function as the "head" of the solo with patterns of harmonized 6ths relative to the E (I), A (IV), and E changes in measures 1–8 and dyads in 3rds for measures 9–12 over the B (V), A, E, and B chords. The combination of the vintage 'burst and the snarky little Supro creates a unique squawking sound not unlike Hubert Sumlin's on the original "Killing Floor."

In measures 13–24, the legendary "Hammer of the Gods" guitarist shows how well he learned his lessons from the Chicago blues masters like Otis Rush and Buddy Guy. He restricts himself to the root-octave position of the E minor pentatonic scale while relying, to a large degree, on his remarkable phrasing to invent a blues world of great drama and emotional expression. Page achieves the result through a variety of means, foremost of which is the contrast between concise licks in quarter-, eighth-, and sixteenth-note rhythms and careening passages fueled mainly by smoking sixteenth notes. This is evident in measures 13–15 over the E chord where he plays relatively "sparsely" while also creating a motif repeated in measures 13 and 15 for structural integrity. In measures 16 and 17, over E and A, he ratchets up the intensity with a classic British blues-rock pattern involving a pull-off and a bend. By measures 18, 19, and 20 over A, E, and E, he is navigating the scale with the speed and handling of a vintage Jaguar XKE. Measures 21–24 over B7, A7, E7, and B7 contain the dynamic contrast of fewer notes, rests, and woozy bends and vibrato.

The third and last chorus of 12-bar blues in measures 25–36 shows the glorious results of "singing" through the guitar as Page works a number of bends off of the root E note at fret 17 on string 2 in measures 25–27. Following the effective approach of the previous 12 measures, Page then gooses the energy level by utilizing an intriguing three-note pull-off in measures 28–32 over the E7, A7, A7, E7, and E7 chords. Containing the G, E, and C♯ notes from the E composite blues scale, it harmonizes and locks in with the A7 change but creates bluesy musical tension over the E chords. Peaking magnificently over the B7 in measure 33 with a cascading series of bends starting from the G note on string 1 that resolves to the root, Page nails the A7 in measure 34 with E and C♯ and then rushes down from E to E for final resolution in measures 35–36 on the E harmony.

Vital Stats

Guitarist: Jimmy Page

Song: "The Lemon Song"

Album: *Led Zeppelin II*

Age at time of recording: 25

Guitar: 1958 Gibson sunburst Les Paul Standard

Amp: Supro 1690T Coronado

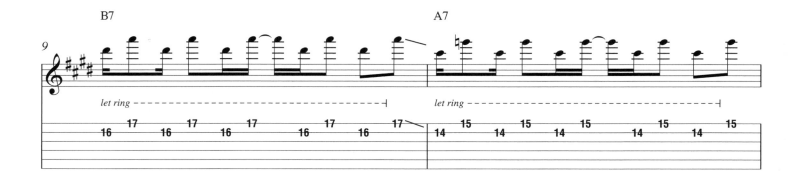

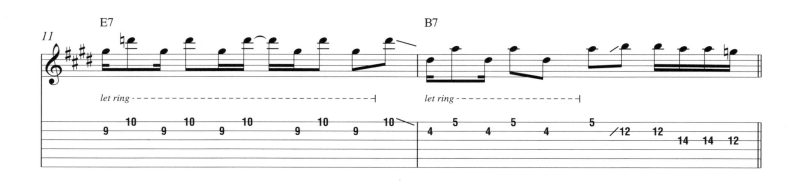

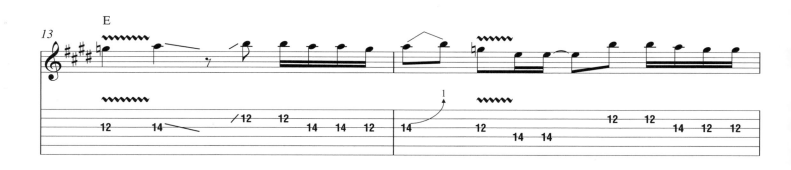

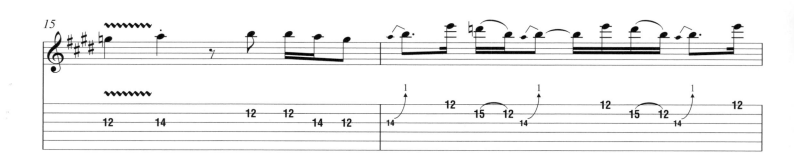

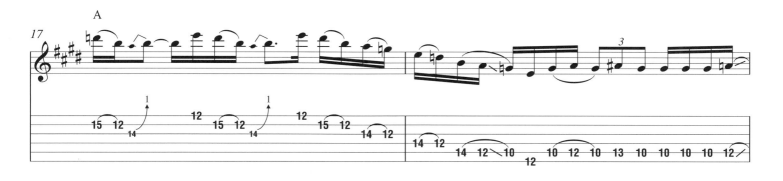

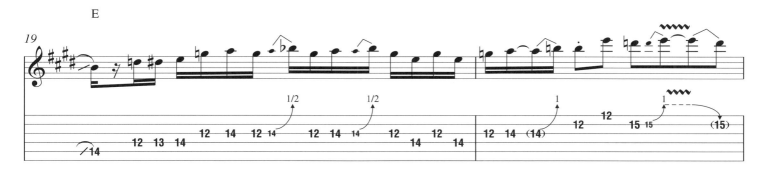

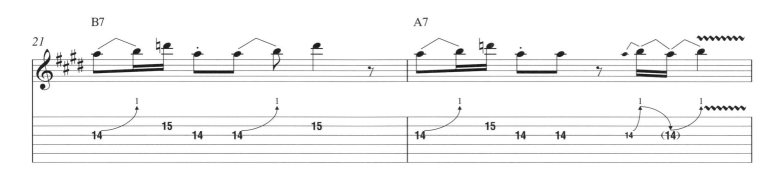

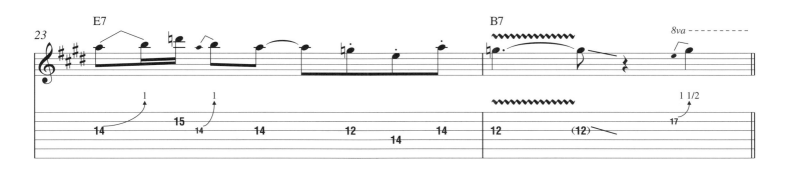

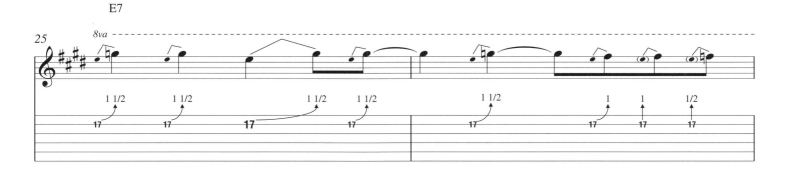

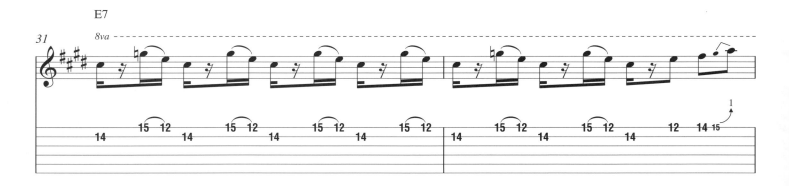

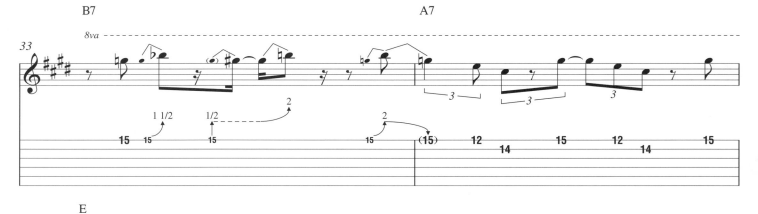

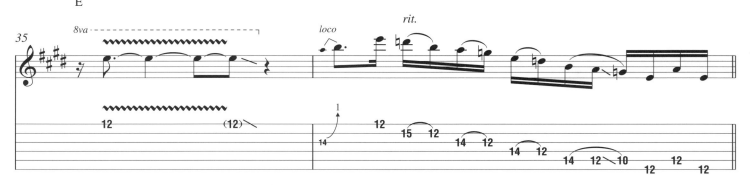

Duane Allman

Nominally a product of the blues revival of the sixties, the Allman Brothers Band transcended the genre as well as the British blues rock of the era. In the process, they became the leading proponent of southern rock, a genre steeped in the blues that features advanced instrumental prowess.

In 1969 in Jacksonville, Florida, session guitarist Duane Allman assembled a band with Jaimoe Johanson (drums), Butch Trucks (drums), Berry Oakley (bass), and Dickey Betts (guitar) after an epic and epochal jam. He realized his "dream" when his brother Gregg returned from California to sing lead and play Hammond B-3 organ on *The Allman Brothers Band* featuring "Whipping Post." *Idlewild South* (#38) in 1970, with "Revival (Love Is Everywhere)" and "In Memory of Elizabeth Reed," showed major artistic growth. The gold *At*

Fillmore East (#13), one of the greatest live albums of all-time, revealed them as ultimate blues and rock improvisers with a jazz sensibility. Then tragedy struck when, half-way through recording *Eat a Peach* (#5), Duane Allman was killed in a motorcycle accident in Macon, Georgia, at the age of 25 on October 29, 1971. Betts finished the guitar parts, and Chuck Leavell was added on keyboards. A second tragedy occurred when Oakley also died in a motorcycle accident on November 11, 1972, not far from where Duane fell; he was replaced by Lamar Williams.

Brothers and Sisters (#1) in 1973, with the signature "Ramblin' Man" (#2), initiated the Dickey Betts era that took the band away from heavy blues into country rock territory and peak popularity. In the summer, they jammed before 600,000 in Watkins Glen, N.Y. They began to unravel, however, with Betts and Gregg releasing solo albums, and the latter's two marriages to Cher. *Win, Lose or Draw* (#5) in 1975 was another hit, but substance abuse was wearing them down. When Gregg testified against a friend in a federal drug case in 1976, the wheels came off. Johanson, Leavell, and Williams left to form Sea Level, and Betts pursued his

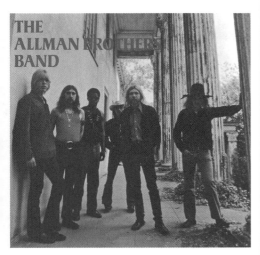

This classic album simultaneously heralded the debut of a great band, a fertile genre, and one of the most spectacular guitar tandems in rock history with Allman and Betts.

"When Lonnie Mack came out with the guitar instrumental 'Memphis' I thought, 'Oh, God, finally something we guitar players can relate to!'"

—Dickey Betts

solo career. The live *Wipe the Windows, Check the Oil, Dollar Gas* (#75) was a stop-gap release, and in 1978, the band made a comeback attempt.

Enlightened Rogues (#9), with "Crazy Love" (#29) in 1979, was encouraging, and the addition of guitarist Dan Toler restored the twin guitar attack. *Reach for the Sky* (#27) and *Brothers of the Road* (#44) with "Straight from the Heart" (#11) in 1980 and 1981, respectively, was essentially the "end of the road" again for the eighties. Williams died in 1983, and Leavell and Johanson went off with the Stones. In 1989, they reformed and were revitalized with the exceptional guitarist Warren Haynes as revealed on *Seven Turns* in 1990. A series of live albums filled out the nineties, as the band was inducted into the Rock and Roll Hall of Fame in 1995 and won a Grammy for "Jessica" in 1996.

Haynes and bassist Allen Woody left in 1997 to form Gov't Mule, while Betts was unceremoniously fired after 30 years in 2000 and temporarily replaced by Jimmy Herring. *Hittin' the Note* (#37) in 2003 showed their new-found strength with bassist Oteil Burbridge and guitarist Derek Trucks, nephew of Butch, complementing Haynes who had returned in 2001. Since 1989, the Brothers have played 175 shows at the Beacon Theater in NYC. Beginning in 2000, they have enjoyed extended runs each spring, though the 2008 dates had to be cancelled due to Greg's bout with hepatitis C. A string of 13 successful shows were held in March of 2009, however, with guests like Johnny Winter and Eric Clapton, to mark the 40th anniversary of the band.

How to Play It

Live versions of "Whipping Post" were epic productions like "Freebird" and became such a cliché that even Frank Zappa was compelled to cover it in response to the requests that were being hurled his way in the seventies. Nonetheless, it stands as a monumental achievement in the Allman Brothers oeuvre and a timeless testament to their uniquely creative talent with blues forms.

The studio version from their debut album, like the subsequent live extravaganzas, is in the unusual time signature (for blues rock) of 6/8 and flashes short solos by Duane and Dickey, respectively. Following the first interlude (not shown), Duane cuts loose with 16 measures of compressed and barely contained energy. Utilizing the same two-measure vamp of A–Bm and C–Bm from the verses, he burns through the A blues scale, with the addition of the B note from the A Mixolydian mode, in the root and extension positions. He was a master of various styles and techniques, including improvising modally over a vamp, and his solo is an outstanding example of the latter as he fashions sheets of musical tension and release.

After establishing his tonality in measure 1 with the sustained and vibratoed root A note, Duane is off and running to wreak audio havoc. Check out the lick in measure 2 where he includes the B note with a gliss from the C over the C and Bm changes, and then builds subtle tension in measures 3–4 by repeating the E note and working his way up the root position of the A minor pentatonic, all the while

avoiding conclusive resolution to any root notes. In measures 5–7, he plays twisted, knotted licks based around a classic blues sound of the D on string 3 at fret 7 bent to E, pulled-off to the C on fret 5, and resolved, albeit quite briefly, to the root A note at fret 7 on string 4. The heightened musical tension is released in measure 8 where Duane plays a slower melodic riff similar to measure 2 but ramped up again in measures 9–11 with the D note repeatedly bent to the E, which harmonizes with the A, Bm, and C chords.

Planning his exit down the line in measure 16, Duane smoothly accelerates up from the root position of the A minor pentatonic scale to the extension position in measures 11–13, capping his run with an elastic bend of D to E that has become a bluesy motif in the solo. In measure 14, he repeats his other motif with a melodic riff similar to measures 2 and 8 over the same chords—the only occasion where the B note from the A Mixolydian mode appears. Measure 15 once again features the D bent to E in the root position of the A minor pentatonic scale followed by a bend of F to G on fret 10. Duane then resolves all previous tension and climaxes his epochal solo with flair in measure 16 by continuing up on string 3 to bend G to A at fret 12.

Vital Stats

Guitarist: Duane Allman

Song: "Whipping Post"

Album: *The Allman Brothers Band*

Age at time of recording: 23

Guitar: Les Paul Standard

Amp: Marshall 50 watt stack

Leslie West

Mountain bridged the late sixties and early seventies by literally "amping up" the blues into Blues Rock 2.0 with brutal riffs and punishing solos. Young headbangers loved the band as the natural evolution from Cream, and the physically "mountainous" guitarist Leslie West assumed iconic status in the genre.

In 1968, West (née Weinstein) was playing in the Vagrants, a Long Island-based R&B band, when they cut a version of Otis Redding's "Respect" (preceding Aretha's hit) for Atlantic Records with producer/guitarist/bassist Felix Pappalardi. They disbanded, and Pappalardi went off to England to produce *Disraeli Gears* with Cream but admonished West to stay in touch. Not coincidentally, West saw Clapton with Cream at the Fillmore East in 1968 and was transfixed.

When Pappalardi returned, West rang him up and presented his new group. Pappalardi took over the bass chair, and with drummer Norman D. Smart and keyboardist Steve Knight in tow, he and West repaired to the studio in 1969 for *Leslie West – Mountain*, which made it to #72 on the charts. They hit the road, and their fourth gig was at Woodstock.

Smart was replaced by Corky Laing just before Mountain's official debut, *Climbing!*, in 1970. Powered by West's full-bore Marshall/Clapton roar, it sold a million copies, climbed to #17, and produced the classic "Mississippi Queen" that sailed to #21. Both *Nantucket Sleighride* and *Flowers of Evil* were released in 1971, with the former gliding to #16 and the latter blossoming at #35. *Mountain Live* in 1972 marked the end of the first incarnation of the band, as Pappalardi cited hearing damage and a desire to produce. Around this time, the Who were recording *Who's Next* in New York, and Pete Townsend asked West to play lead on several tracks so as not to need overdubs, though eventually his contribution was wiped away.

West fired Knight, and he and Laing joined vocalist Paul Rodgers from Free, along with guitarist Mick Ralphs, and bassist Overend Watts from Mott the Hoople in a new venture. While rehearsing in London, Jack Bruce stopped by to jam, and West pursued the dream of a power trio. West, Bruce, and Laing created three albums before Bruce split in 1973, while Rodgers and Ralphs formed Bad Company.

© Getty

"Great tone is like pornography. You're not sure what it is, but you know it when you hear it."

—Leslie West

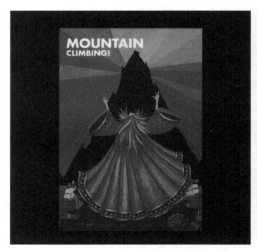

The "Great Fatsby" dwarfed his plank-like LP Jr., but his gargantuan tone and granite riffs scaled the heights of blues rock ecstasy.

West and Laing continued as Leslie West's Wild West Show and then welcomed back Pappalardi along with keyboardist Bob Mann in the new Mountain for the live double album, *Twin Peaks* in 1973. Guitarist David Perry replaced Mann in 1974 for *Avalanche*. Following that breakup, West included Laing in the Leslie West Band for *The Great Fatsby* (1975) and *Phantom* a year later, which included guitarist Mick Jones (before he founded Foreigner).

As happens, substance abuse caught up with West, and he lay low into the eighties. Pappalardi was shot dead in 1983 by his wife Gail Collins, but in 1985, West again rebuilt Mountain with Laing and Brit bassist Mark Clarke on *Go for Your Life*. After that breakup, Jack Bruce returned "one time only" in 1988 for *Theme*. West went forward as a solo act with *Alligator* in 1989, featuring fusion bassist Stanley Clarke, followed by *Leslie West Live* and *Dodgin' the Dirt* in 1993. The next year, Laing rejoined West along with bassist Noel Redding for a touring version of Mountain. West, Laing, and Mark Clarke recorded *Man's World* as Mountain in 1996, and West continued slimming down for his solo effort *As Phat as It Gets* in 1999. In 2002, West and Laing, with bassist Chuck Hearne, tracked *Mystic Fire*. West released *Blues to Die For* with Gunter Nezhoda and Aynsley Dunbar in 2003, *Gitarded* with various guests in 2004, *Got Blooze* with Tim Bogart and Dunbar in 2005, *Blue Me* in 2006 with Tim Fahey and Dunbar, and *Masters of War* in 2007 with Laing.

How to Play It

With one of the most recognizable and downright nastiest tones in classic blues rock, Leslie West channels B.B. King through Eric Clapton to produce a modern masterpiece. Early electric blues guitarists in the forties and fifties distorted their amps in an attempt to compete with and capture the big, raw sound of the braying saxophone, and West does an admirable job replicating it sonically in concert with his fluid phrasing.

The 16-measure solo consists of measures 1–8 in E (I) from the chorus combined with measures 1–8 (A and E) from the verse before singer/bassist Felix Pappalardi resumes singing (not shown). West rocks out in two positions of the E minor pentatonic scale along with a brief visit to the root position of the C# minor pentatonic scale functioning as the E major pentatonic. Dig that his signature lick throughout "Mississippi Queen" is reprised in measures 1–4 where he executes a classic B.B. King move in the affectionately named "B.B. King box" played at fret 17. Be aware that the bend from F# to G# (major 3rd) at fret 19 on string 2 and the inclusion of the C# note on string 3 at fret 18 in measure 2 are actually found in the E major pentatonic scale. The bend to the G# blended with the B note on string 1 at fret 19 creates a strong E major tonality and should be played by bending with the ring finger backed up by the middle and index fingers. Use the pinky for the B note.

Do not miss the striking and honking half-step bend of C/F# on beat 4 of measure 7 dramatically sustained across the bar line to beat 1 of measure 8. It is derived from the C# minor pentatonic scale where West resides temporarily in order to resolve conclusively to the root E on string 3 at fret 9 with sassy index finger vibrato, paying homage to the "King of the Blues." In measures 9–12, where the harmony advances to the A (IV) chord, West sidles into the root-octave position of the E minor pentatonic scale and emphasizes the A note to acknowledge the chord change like a good bluesman.

When the chords change back to E beginning in measure 13, West resumes his inspired improvisation in the "B.B. King box" at fret 17. His Les Paul Junior (with the brawny P-90 single coil pickup) really sings out in this range, and he takes full advantage of the situation by focusing his attention on the F# note on string 2 at fret 19 bent one step to the sweet G# (major 3rd) that functions as a motif throughout the solo. Observe that, after resolving to the root E note with vibrato in measure 14, West decides to climax his solo straight into the vocal section with a bravura performance of precise, repeating, lyrical, whole-step bends of B to C# at fret 19 on string 1 to produce the likewise sweet 6th like an alto saxophone.

Vital Stats

Guitarist: Leslie West

Song: "Mississippi Queen"

Album: *Climbing!* – Mountain

Age at time of recording: 25

Guitar: Late '50s Les Paul Junior

Amp: Marshall 100 watt stack

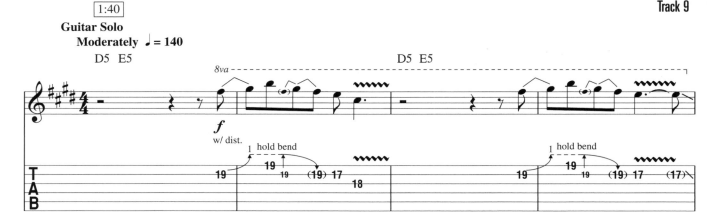

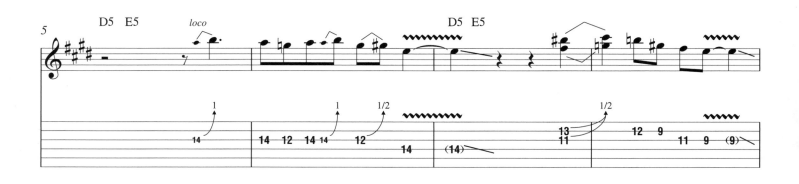

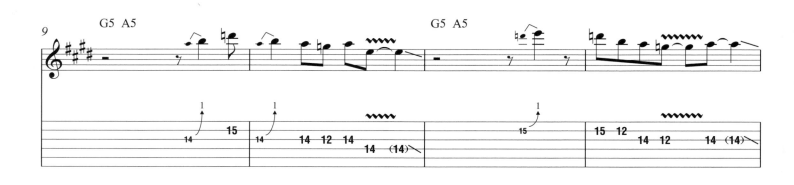

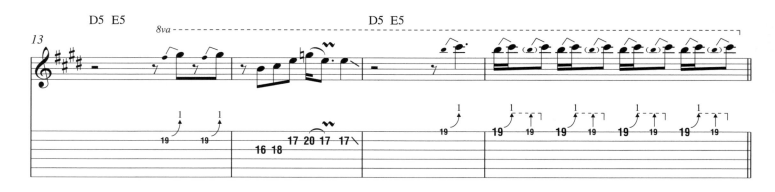

Words and Music by Leslie West, Felix Pappalardi, Corky Laing and David Rea
Copyright © 1970 by Universal Music - MGB Songs
Copyright Renewed
International Copyright Secured   All Rights Reserved

Tony Iommi

Though the bullying blues rock of Led Zeppelin and Deep Purple are often inaccurately described as the precursors of heavy metal, Black Sabbath was actually ground zero for the sound and attitude. Their bludgeoning riffs, "metallic" guitar tone, "paranoid" demonic lyrics, and howling vocals have influenced all succeeding metalheads.

In 1968, guitarist Anthony "Tony" Iommi and drummer William "Bill" Ward from Mythology formed a blues rock group with bassist Terence "Geezer" Butler and singer John "Ozzy" Osbourne from Rare Breed. Originally called the Polka Tulk Blues Company, followed by Polka Tulk, and then Earth, they played Cream, Hendrix, and Blue Cheer covers in clubs throughout Europe. However, Iommi split to join Jethro Tull until early 1969. They discovered a band with a similar name and, with a combination of seeing the Boris Karloff movie,

Ground zero for heavy metal also contained serious anti-war commentary in addition to head-banging riffs.

Black Sabbath, and Butler reading occult literature and writing a song called "Black Sabbath," it led to the fortuitous name change. An aesthetic and commercial decision was made to focus on dark, satanic subjects and horror.

Black Sabbath was released on Friday the 13th, 1970, and sold a million copies while incanting at #23. The landmark *Paranoid* (1971) hit #1 in England and #12 in the U.S. with sales in excess of four million; the driving title track hit #61, and the molten sludge of "Iron Man" grinded to #52. *Master of Reality* (#8 in 1971) and *Black Sabbath Vol. 4* (#13 in 1972) led to *Sabbath, Bloody Sabbath* (#11 in 1973) with keyboardist wizard Rick Wakeman from Yes guesting in a move that would begin to sow the seeds of dissent despite it being their

© Marty Temme

fifth straight million-selling album. There followed a protracted period of inactivity due to rampant substance abuse and internal and management squabbles.

"The Manhattan Federal Court suit also charges that Osbourne's 'signature lead vocals' are largely responsible for the band's 'extraordinary success,' noting that its popularity plummeted during his absence from 1980 through 1996."

—Part of the suit brought by Ozzy Osbourne against Tony Iommi

When *Sabotage* (1975) failed to generate the success of previous albums, their record company rush-released *We Sold Our Soul for Rock 'n' Roll*, a two-disc compilation that sold a million copies. *Technical Ecstasy* (1976) contained the expanded instrumentation and production that Iommi favored but failed to excite the audience sufficiently, and Osbourne quit in 1977. A year later, he was back for *Never Say Die!*, only to leave for a solo career in 1979.

Singer Ronnie James Dio of Rainbow fame slipped into his place from 1980–83, after which he left with drummer Vinnie Appice, who had been brought in when Bill Ward left in 1981 for "health reasons." Ward was convinced to return as Ian Gillan, formerly of Deep Purple, was hired for *Born Again*, generally considered to be the low point for the Sabs. Gillan rejoined the Purps in 1984, and Osbourne came back for Live Aid in 1985. He and bassist Butler left afterwards as the band became Iommi's personal domain with various singers and bassists before he brought back the complete Dio aggregation through 1992.

The musical chairs continued until 1997 when a mostly live double-disc set, *Reunion*, was produced with all four original members. A platinum-seller in the U.S., it gained a Grammy for "Iron Man." Two tours followed, including an appearance at Ozzfest, and plans were made in 2001 for the first album of new material since 1978, but a session with trendy producer Rick Rubin ended all hope when Osbourne left to complete a solo album. He would go on to have a hit reality TV show in 2002, and the band was inducted into the Rock and Roll Hall of Fame in 2006. In 2007, Iommi and Dio reunited in a band called Heaven and Hell with ongoing tours and recordings.

How to Play It

Tony Iommi used a Dallas Rangemaster Treble Booster to help create his unique steely and raunchy tone on one of the founding solos of heavy metal music that is as fluid as the underlying rhythm is chunky. The left-handed power chord purveyor lost the tips of his middle and ring fingers on his right hand at work when he was 17. However, he managed to keep playing by going to extra light strings and using leather-covered plastic thimbles for his damaged fingertips. The result has been rock immortality for the instrumental voice of doom behind Black Sabbath.

Iommi uses the E minor pentatonic scale to make his historic musical statement in the 16-measure guitar solo. Over the four-measure progression from the verse (not shown) of E5, E5, D5, and G5–D5–E5–Em7 repeated four times, he smoothly navigates four positions of the scale with fluid bends, pull-offs, and hammer-ons. As expected in a modal solo such as "Paranoid," he produces interest and forward momentum by creating tension through a variety of means and then releasing it to the E root note. Measure 1 contains one of the most basic ways to achieve this approach with a robust bend at fret 9 on string 3 of one-and-a-half steps from E to G that is released quickly back to E, pulled off to the D, and hammered to the vibratoed E that dramatically crosses the bar line into measure 2. In a brilliant strategic move, Iommi then builds cool tension by avoiding the root note in measures 3–4 and only touching on it briefly in measures 5–7.

Beginning in measure 8, he makes a slick move up to the root-octave position of the E minor pentatonic scale at fret 12 where the vast majority of blues and blues-based

rock guitarists like to hang out. Notice, however, that Iommi, despite his early experience, has removed most vestiges of the blues from his phrasing in part from the fact that he does not employ any rests throughout the entire solo. Even classic licks like the one over beats 3 and 4 of measure 8 are played in straight eighth notes without syncopation instead of a triplet that would make it swing. Likewise, the spiky bends of G to A on string 1 at fret 15 in measures 9 and 10 are many miles removed from Albert King, though they do emphasize the metallurgical sound of the ominous Rangemaster/Laney combination for peak tension.

Looking ahead to the finish line, Iommi reverses direction starting in measure 11 and through to measure 16, as he descends down the root-octave position with quick resolution to the root E note on string 4 at fret 14 at least once every measure. One of his favorite methods of dynamically achieving that worthy goal is by bending the A note to B on string 3 at fret 14 and then pulling off from A to G before nailing the E note, as shown in measures 12 and 13. Be hip that this is a common blues maneuver, but Iommi executes it so quickly and evenly within the unbroken string of notes that it registers mainly in the subconscious as a minor bit of musical turbulence.

Vital Stats

Guitarist: Tony Iommi

Song: "Paranoid"

Album: *Paranoid* – Black Sabbath

Age at time of recording: 22

Guitar: 1965 Gibson SG Special w/ John Birch custom single coil in bridge

Amp: Laney Supergroup LA. 100BL

Elliot Randall

© Neil Zlozower

"The solo on 'Reeling in the Years' is my favorite of all-time."

—Jimmy Page

Before Steely Dan, studio bands were at the beck and call of autocratic producers. The "Wrecking Crew" of Los Angeles studio fame and the "Funk Brothers" at Motown in the sixties come immediately to mind. The Dan, however, occasionally gigged and was guided by two renegade musicians with a sophisticated vision of rock, pop, jazz, and R&B that allowed their "sidemen," particularly the guitarists, to blow with intense brilliance in the recording studio.

Walter Becker (bass and guitar) and Donald Fagen (keyboards) met at Bard College in upstate New York in 1967 and were soon playing an eclectic mix of jazz and rock in a number of local bands. In time, they began writing songs together with the goal of becoming hired pros in the manner of Carole King and Gerry Goffin who toiled on Broadway in the famous Brill Building of New York City in the late fifties and early sixties. Starting in 1970, they paid their dues in the backup band of Jay & the Americans, which also contained guitarist Elliot Randall, and contributed the soundtrack to a low-budget film and a Barbra Streisand song in 1971. A move to the Big Apple precipitated their fortuitous meeting with producer Gary Katz who snared them a position as staff writers at ABC/Dunhill Records in Los Angeles, convinced them to start their own band in order to promote their music, and would

remain an influence. Taking their name from a dildo mentioned in William Burroughs' *Naked Lunch*, they enlisted guitarists Jeff "Skunk" Baxter and Denny Dias along with drummer Jim Hodder and vocalist/keyboardist David Palmer in 1972.

Can't Buy a Thrill borrowed its title from Bob Dylan's "It Takes a Lot to Laugh (It Takes a Train to Cry)" and made an audacious debut at #17. "Reeling in the Years" and "Do It Again" (#6) would go on to become FM radio classics and gave little hint of the jazzier direction they would eventually take. A disastrous tour revealed the inherent problems of an under-rehearsed band playing "brainy" pop rock for an audience wanting to boogie. Following the harder rocking *Countdown to Ecstasy* (#35 in 1973) and *Pretzel Logic* (#8 in 1974), with "Rikki Don't Lose That Number" at #4 (rumored to be about Rick Derringer) that featured new lead vocalist Michael McDonald and drummer Jeff Porcaro, Becker and Fagen decided to retire from live performances. Through 1980, they

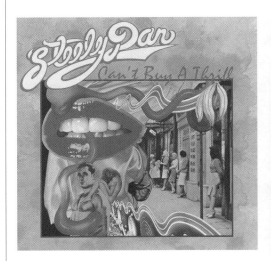

"Reeling in the Years" still thrills, begging the request to "Do It Again."

followed their muse in an increasingly jazzy vein with the classics of fusion *Katy Lied* (#13 in 1975), *The Royal Scam* (#15 in 1976), *Aja* (#3 in 1977), and *Gaucho* (#9 in 1980), all containing exceptional guitarists like Baxter, Dias, Elliot Randall, Larry Carlton, and other noted L.A. studio royalty (including Rick Derringer).

Despite their increasingly critical and commercial success, Becker and Fagen called it quits, going their separate, solo ways until 1993 when Becker produced *Kamakiriad* for Fagen in conjunction with the first Steely Dan tour since 1974. The positive response to the tour and the accompanying live album, *Alive in America* (#40), resulted in a second tour in 1995 and a Becker/Fagen collaboration, *Two Against Nature*, in 2000 that won the Grammy for Album of the Year. In 2001, they were inducted into the Rock and Roll Hall of Fame. *Everything Must Go*, the first new Steely Dan album in over twenty years, was released in 2003 as Becker and Fagen followed with new solo projects, as well. In 2008, another Dan tour was mounted.

How to Play It

On "Reeling in the Years," Elliot Randall was truly "in the zone"—that mystical place where musicians and athletes operate at peak efficiency on an almost subconscious level. Remarkably, he was able to maintain undiminished creativity for all three of his sensational solos and,

given the strength shown on the fade out (not shown), he sounds as if he could have gone on riffing indefinitely. It also appears that his choice of gear was fortuitous, as the humbucker added to his Strat through the atypical choice of the overdriven Ampeg bass amp allowed him to squeeze and sustain creamy treble tones and force bass notes to growl like a honking R&B alto saxophonist.

The 16-measure intro solo is also a fine "introduction" to Randall's exceedingly tasty style and approach that is partially defined by his intuitive sense of dynamic contrast between treble and bass. With unerring intuition, he glides from high-to-low and low-to-high registers while emitting great exuberance. Over a simple rock vamp of G and A major chords for two measures each, he manages to suggest the vocal melody, imbue the progression with an immediate jolt of energy, and phrase with delirious abandon. Though the key signature is D major notated as A Mixolydian, Randall plays as if in the key of A major with his "secret" weapon: the A composite blues scale (blues scale combined with Mixolydian mode) and the G major scale, as opposed to noodling in the more common A minor pentatonic scale. The glorious result is a melodic solo with just enough bluesy attitude to give it a pungent flavor.

Dig how Randall "sings" through his Strat, "Are you reeling in the years, stowin' away the time" from the chorus, in the pickup and measures 1–3 for one of the most indelible entrances in rock history. He then continues in the A composite blues scale through measure 8, picking notes to also harmonize over the

G chords where appropriate. Along the way, notice how he definitely acknowledges the A change in measures 7 and 8 with the A/F♯ dyad and an A major arpeggio, respectively. Following with a similar concept in measures 9–10 over the G chord, he literally changes keys and slips into the G major scale via an arpeggiated first-inversion G major triad at fret 3 and then dynamically slithers up an octave to fret 15. Measures 11–12 of the A change contain one of the signature moves of the song as Randall skips lightly and gracefully down string 1 with glisses and pull-offs starting at fret 14 on F♯, hitting every note from the A Mixolydian mode down to the open 1st string. He then cleverly repeats the G note on beat 1 of measure 13 over the G chord and once there, reverts back to the G major scale into measure 14, using a cool ascending line from B to D on string 5 to walk the solo back to A in measures 15 and 16. With utter finality, Randall concludes his opening salvo with a fat, sustained open-position A power chord in measure 16.

Vital Stats

Guitarist: Elliot Randall

Song: "Reeling in the Years"

Album: *Can't Buy a Thrill –* Steely Dan

Age at time of recording: 25

Guitar: 1963 Fender Stratocaster with Gibson PAF humbucker in neck position

Amp: Ampeg SVT bass amp

*Key signature denotes A Mixolydian.

Words and Music by Walter Becker and Donald Fagen
Copyright © 1972, 1973 UNIVERSAL MUSIC CORP. and RED GIANT, INC.
Copyrights Renewed
All Rights Controlled and Administered by UNIVERSAL MUSIC CORP.
All Rights Reserved   Used by Permission

Ritchie Blackmore

Deep Purple has been cited by the *Guinness Book of World Records* for being the world's "loudest rock band" and for having most guitarists play their "Smoke on the Water" riff. Sometimes lost in the crush of enthusiasm for the riff, however, is the overwhelming power of axe-slinger Ritchie Blackmore's soaring solo.

In Hertford, England, in 1967, Blackmore, Rod Evans (vocals), Jon Lord (keyboards), Nick Simper (bass), and Ian Paice (drums) formed Roundabout. Originally the backup band for ex-Searchers drummer Chris Curtis, they separated before their 1968 debut album, *Shades of Deep Purple* (#24), and changed their name in honor of the pop standard that was a favorite of Blackmore's grandmother. It contained a progressive rock version of Joe South's "Hush" (#4), while the follow-up, The *Book of Taliesyn* (#54) in 1969, featured Neil Diamond's "Kentucky Woman" (#38) along with other covers done in the over-wrought "baroque" style espoused by Vanilla Fudge. Their self-titled third release showed the classical influence of organist Lord even as Evans and Simper were replaced by Ian Gillan and Roger Glover to create the beloved classic lineup.

© Marty Temme

Concerto for Group and Orchestra in 1969 was a live collaboration with the Royal Philharmonic Orchestra that stiffed, convincing Blackmore to take the wheel from Lord and steer the band in a snarling, rock guitar direction. The result was the million-selling *Deep Purple in Rock* in 1970 that pounded long and hard. Though it did not break the Top 100, along with *Fireball* (#32) the following year, it set the pace for the Purp's rule as rock titans in the early seventies. The benchmark was *Machine Head* (#7) in 1972, followed by the incendiary *Live in Japan* (#6), which put them in company with Led Zeppelin and Black Sabbath courtesy of "Highway Star," "Space Truckin'," and especially "Smoke on the Water" (#4). Based on a true story, it documented the burning of the historic Montreux casino in Switzerland and the extraordinary effort necessary to complete the song and album.

Though *Who Do We Think We Are!* (#15) in 1973, with "Woman from Tokyo" (#60), maintained their momentum, the wheels started to come off. Gillan left

The title is a wry take on metal music, but could also refer to the tuners on Blackmore's axe that get thoroughly tested throughout.

> *"I'm very moved by Renaissance music, but I still love to play hard rock—though only if it's sophisticated and has some thought behind it."*
>
> —Ritchie Blackmore

after a long-simmering conflict with Blackmore, and Glover soon followed. Singer David Coverdale and bassist/singer Glen Hughes were brought in for *Burn* (#9) in 1974, which benefited from the alternating lead vocals of the new recruits. Alas, it would not last. Blackmore split in 1975 to form Rainbow with vocalist Ronnie James Dio following *Stormbringer* (#20). Ex-James Gang guitar ace Tommy Bolin played his heart out on *Come Taste the Band* (#43) in 1975, but after a farewell tour, Deep Purple pulled the plug in 1976.

A reunion with the classic lineup occurred in 1984 for the platinum *Perfect Strangers* (#17), *The House of Blue Light* (#34) in 1987, and *Nobody's Perfect* the following year. From there on, the band became the proverbial revolving door with Gillan and Blackmore quitting at regular intervals. Vocalist Joe Lynn Turner appeared on *Slaves and Masters* in 1990, while Gillan returned for *The Battle Rages On...* in 1992, though Blackmore quit midway through the tour and was replaced by Joe Satriani. In 1994, Steve Morse signed on, though Blackmore appeared on *Stranger in Us All* in 1995, and he played on *Purpendicular* in 1996, *Abandon* in 1998, and *Live at the Royal Albert Hall* in 2000. Meanwhile, Blackmore formed the Renaissance-based Blackmore's Night in 1997 with his fiancé and singer Candace Night, releasing eight albums to date of idiosyncratic folk music that is a far cry from Purple and Rainbow.

How to Play It

Ritchie Blackmore checks his massive ego and requisite chops at the door and "marshals" all his musical resources to perform a solo that gains its lasting power from the tastiest of intelligent licks and his vocal-like phrasing.

The 28-measure solo in the key of G minor is mainly constructed from a series of four-measure chord changes: G5, G5, C5, and G5 repeated four times, C5, C5, F5, and F5, and G5 for eight concluding measures. With exquisite control, Blackmore phrases in graceful two-measure increments that show great variety. He establishes his tonality in measures 1 and 2 with the root G note at the twelfth position of the G minor pentatonic scale and then wisely indicates the change to C in measure 3 by bending the B♭ up one step to the root C. In measure 4, he smoothly defines the G chord with a fluid run on string 3 containing notes from the G composite blues scale (Mixolydian mode plus blues scale).

In measures 5 and 6, Blackmore displays his advanced improvisational skills by working in the eighth position of the G scale and transitioning conveniently at the same position to the C composite blues scale in measure 7 with dynamic, syncopated sixteenth-note runs. He follows seamlessly with melodic lines from the G major scale, or Ionian mode, in measure 8 in fifth position. Measures 9–12 find Blackmore for the first time in the common root position of the G blues scale altered to suggest the G Dorian mode, which is best seen in measure 11 over the C chord where he phrases in rippling sixteenth notes similar to measure 7. Be aware that a minor mode,

such as Dorian, is often used over a "power chord" that is theoretically neither major nor minor.

Measures 13–16 show Blackmore cruising up the fingerboard from the root position to the extension position of the G minor pentatonic scale in measures 13–14 over the G chord, from the root position of the C minor pentatonic scale over the C change in measure 15, and to the extension position of the same scale over the G chord in measure 16. Check out how he literally "bends" the scale form to do his bidding, regarding the harmony, by pushing the F note on string 1 at fret 13 up one step to G in measure 16. Measures 17–20 take a new path harmonically with C and F changes, respectively. They constitute a dramatic shift in the harmonic arc of the progression as the band sustains whole notes for each change, and Blackmore moves from the G minor pentatonic at fret 13 to the root and extension positions. He comes back with a swooping bend of C to D into measures 21–22 over the G chord and repeating it while lowering the pitch by degrees as the climax and stuttering "signature" sound of the solo through to measure 23 where he sustains and vibratos the F as the bluesy ♭7th in measure 24. It creates great anticipation, which Blackmore satisfies by returning to the memorable signature riff of the song in measures 25–28.

Vital Stats

Guitarist: Richie Blackmore

Song: "Smoke on the Water"

Album: *Machine Head* – Deep Purple

Age at time of recording: 27

Guitar: Fender Stratocaster

Amp: Marshall 100 watt stack

Smoke on the Water

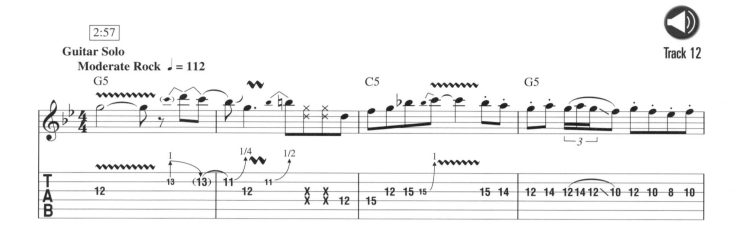

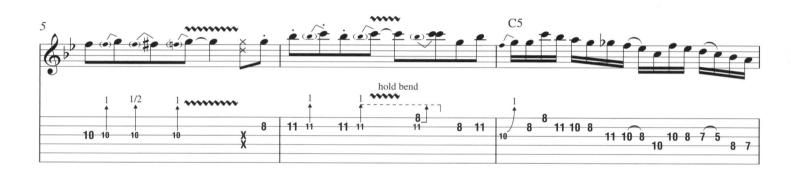

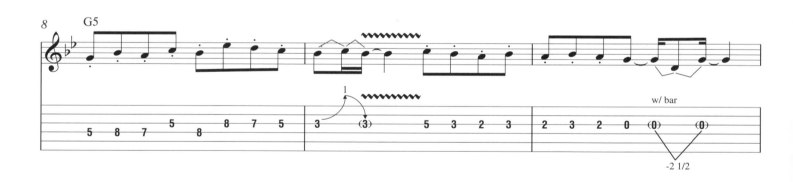

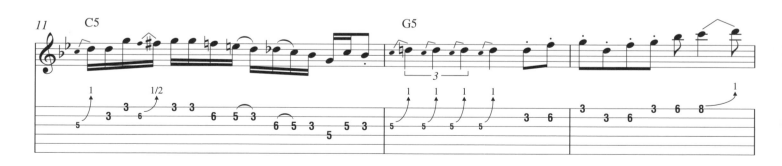

Words and Music by Ritchie Blackmore, Ian Gillan, Roger Glover, Jon Lord and Ian Paice
© 1972 (Renewed 2000) B. FELDMAN & CO. LTD. trading as HEC MUSIC
All Rights for the United States and Canada Controlled and Administered by GLENWOOD MUSIC CORP.

David Gilmour

Pink Floyd navigated the winds of change that blew through rock music from the mid-sixties to the nineties despite two major changes of personnel. The long, strange trip absorbed a rich

"Where would rock 'n' roll be without feedback?"

—David Gilmour

variety of styles from blues to early psychedelia, folk, jazz, and electronica, ultimately creating a unique form of moody, grandiose music.

In Cambridge, England, in 1965, guitarist and singer Syd Barrett joined bassist Roger Waters, keyboardist Rick Wright, and drummer Nick Mason in a British R&B band. An acknowledged genius, Barrett renamed them Pink Floyd in honor of American bluesmen Pinkney "Pink" Anderson and Floyd Council. Under his leadership, they soon evolved into the premier British psychedelic band with mind-blowing light shows and experimental instrumental sound effects.

Their 1967 debut album, *The Piper at the Gates of Dawn*, made the British Top 10 and was hailed as second only to *Sgt. Pepper's* as a psychedelic landmark via Barrett's innovative, rocking, spacey, and humorous songwriting. However, touring revealed his LSD abuse and consequently erratic behavior. In early 1968, David Gilmour, an old classmate, was hired to cover for him on lead guitar, but within months, Barrett's mental condition became so deteriorated that he left to become a solo artist with two albums. Eventually, he was confined to home care by his mother.

Waters assumed lead vocals and writing duties on Floyd's next album, *Saucerful of Secrets*. Combined with Gilmour's impressive skills, it extended and expanded upon the space travel themes of their debut. *More* in 1969 was conceived as a soundtrack for the French hippie movie of the same name. *Ummagumma* followed with a live disc and a studio disc that presented the band in all its otherworldly power, glory, and creativity, charting at #74. *Atom Heart Mother* (1970) at #55 further tantalized with orchestral pretensions and shorter pop material. *Meddle* (1971), with Gilmour taking a larger role on lead vocals and guitar, went to #70 and ended the first chapter of the Pink Floyd saga. *Obscured by Clouds* in 1972 was another movie soundtrack that proved their growing popular appeal at #46. Nothing, however, prepared the band, their fans, or critics for the unprecedented commercial success of *Dark Side of the Moon* the following year. Rocketing to #1, it would remain on the charts for an amazing 741 weeks while raising their status as superstars worldwide; it remains one of the most popular albums in rock history.

Rather than building on the positive elements of *Dark Side of the Moon* in the single "Money," *Wish You Were Here*

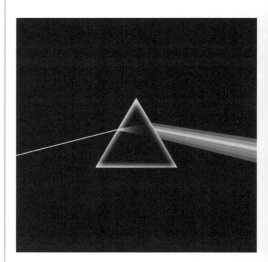

The vastly underrated David Gilmour bent his strings as effortlessly as the pyramid bending light on the album cover.

(1975) reflected Waters' morose tendencies but still went to #1, while the even darker *Animals* (1977) went to #3. *The Wall* (1979) topped out at #1 while being a vehicle for Waters' bleak personality. Though highlighting the most successful chapter of Pink Floyd with long, dirge-like songs, conflicts with Waters preceded their eventual collapse. After the disappointing *The Final Cut* (1983), the band broke up. In 1986, Waters sued Gilmour and Mason when they attempted to reform, but lost. With Gilmour running the show, Pink Floyd-minus-Waters returned. *Momentary Lapse of Reason* was triumphant at #3 in 1987 with Tony Levin on bass and recalled their classic early seventies sound. In what must have been galling to Waters, who was plodding along with a solo career, they hit #1 in 1994 with *The Division Bell*, which also included Wright. Several extravagant tours and live albums were produced in the nineties, along with the significant Floyd reunion at Live 8 in 2005 and their induction into the Rock and Roll Hall of Fame in 2006. Gilmour and Waters have since pursued solo careers, while Barrett died in 2006 at 60 and Wright followed in 2008 at 65.

How to Play It

David Gilmour does not allow his severely overdriven guitar tone to literally "bloom" into outright feedback in his epic "Money" solo. However, he does push it near the limit, giving him long, sensuous sustain to express his dramatic and cathartic improvisation that is a landmark in the Pink Floyd repertoire.

His 70-measure "opus de rock" is comprised of minor key blues changes in three discrete sections of 24, 24, and 22 measures containing Bm7 (i7), Em7 (iv7), and F#m7 (v7) chords. In the first section, Gilmour comes in blazing with the B minor pentatonic scale in the root and extension positions. His bends and fluttering vibrato combine "West Side of Chicago blues" aggression with his own refined sense of melody. As he does throughout the entire solo, Gilmour flows gracefully over and around the chords with unerring note placement and musical space. Check out how he emphasizes the D (♭3rd) in measure 1 and the A (♭7th) notes in measure 2 to create musical anticipation while complementing the minor 7th tonality of the chord change, followed by measures 3–8 where he nails the B root note on string 2 at fret 12 for resolution. In measures 9–24, Gilmour makes sure to nick the root notes of the Em7 and F#m7 chords to add logic and structure to his solo. Pay attention that measures 17–18 contain a dramatic, descending run from the B Aeolian mode that also appears in measures 43–44 and 67–68 as a motif.

Measures 25–48 (the second section) represent a dynamic change as Gilmour ditches the deep reverb and delay in favor of a "dry," more "intimate" sound that nonetheless growls with convincingly authentic blues licks and phrasing. Though he has less sustain due to lowered volume and overdrive, he still executes a series of swooping and soaring bends in measures 35–36, 39, and 41–42 that sound like a baying hound on the bayou. In measures 47–48, a fluid change in tone back to the cavernous deep reverb and delay of the first section occurs as he gathers up all his resources for the concluding and climactic third section of his solo in measures 49–70.

In measure 50, Gilmour literally takes his solo to a higher plain with sub-orbital bends of E to F# at fret 22 on string 1. He follows in measure 52 with a classic B.B. King harmony bend an octave higher than Lucille's friend ever imagined for a violin-like tone that is thrilling to behold. Check out that he resolves the glorious tension in measures 53 and 55 with sustained and vibratoed root notes while utilizing the B as the 5th of Em in measure 57 for subtle musical tension. Gilmour then raises the ante on his solo as he heads to its conclusion with additional screaming bends at fret 22. Included is the B.B. King bend in measures 59 and 62 that serves as yet another motif. Fitting closure is then provided in measures 67–68, where the descending line found in the first two sections of the solo is repeated. Measures 69 and 70 function as a buffer and transition back to the verse, as Gilmour simply plays the root B and F#/D dyads, respectively, to complete the resolution to the Bm tonality.

Vital Stats

Guitarist: David Gilmour

Song: "Money"

Album: *Dark Side of the Moon* – Pink Floyd

Age at time of recording: 27

Guitar: 1970 Bill Lewis 24-fret solidbody electric

Amp: Hiwatt 100 watt head with WEM 4x12 cabinets

Guitar Solo
Moderate Rock ♩ = 118

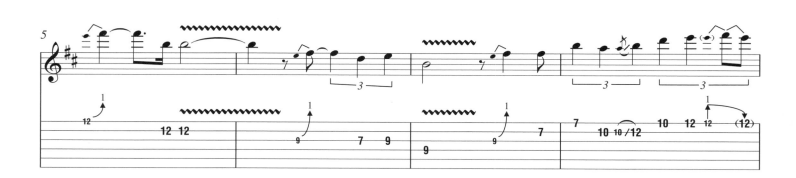

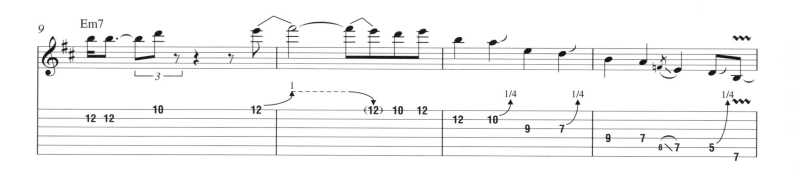

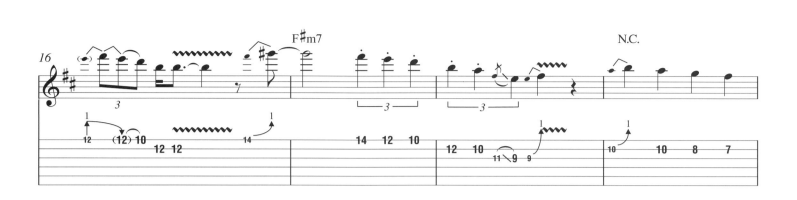

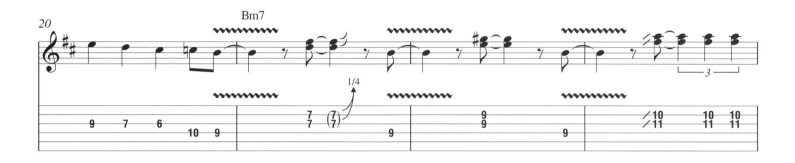

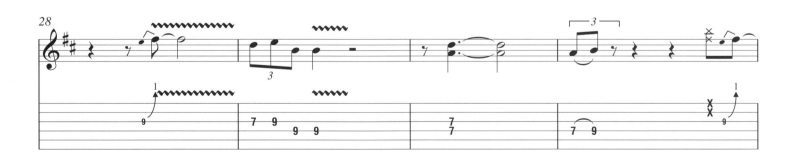

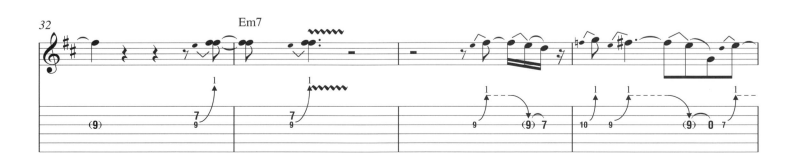

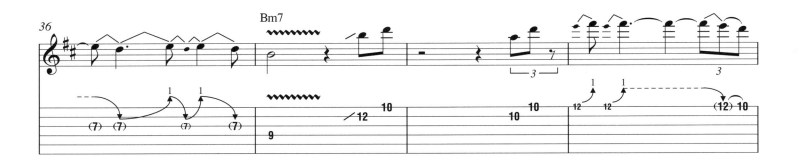

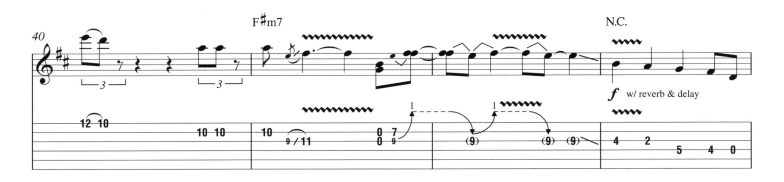

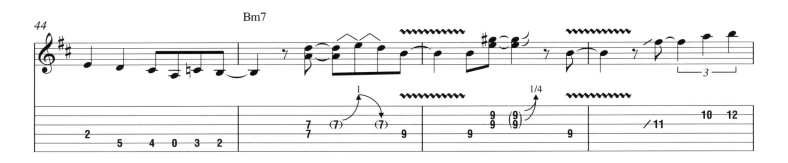

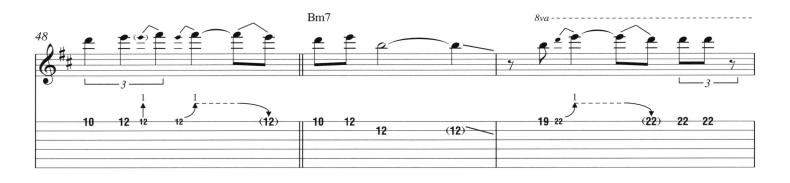

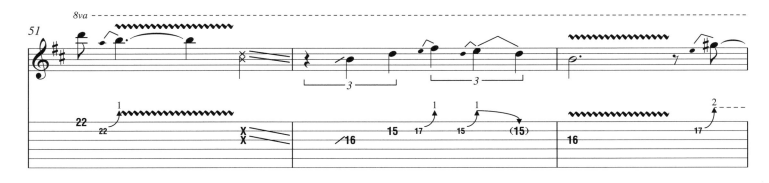

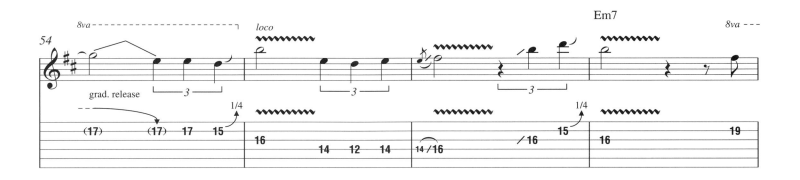

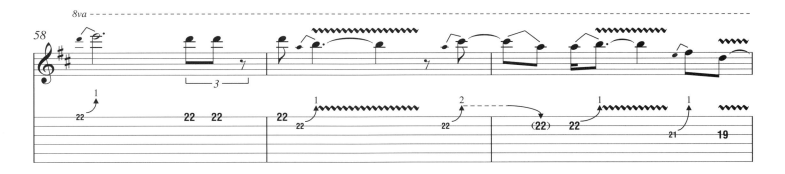

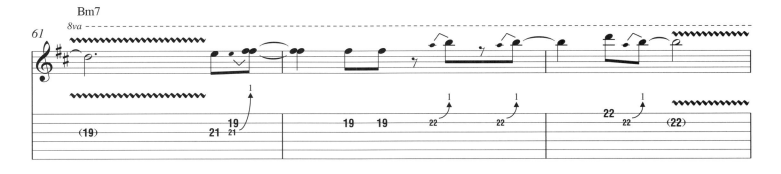

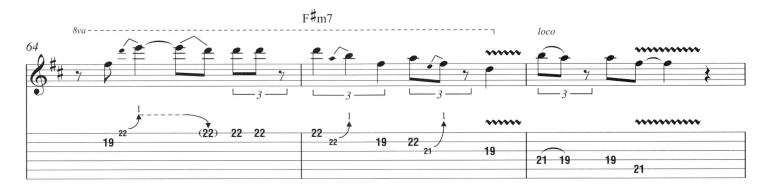

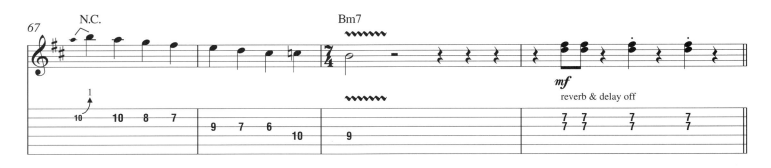

George Kooymans

© Retna

"Brenda Lee's 'Comin' On Strong'"

—Lyric in "Radar Love" referring to a Brenda Lee song often heard on the jukebox in 1966 by Golden Earring vocalist/co-writer Barry Hay when his mother worked at a bar in The Hague

Their unparalleled and unbroken longevity as a pop band tends to negate their "one hit wonder" status. "Radar Love," the biggest certifiable classic rock hit created by Golden Earring, the modern Dutch "masters," however, is uniquely original, haunting, and timeless and has spawned 300 plus covers.

The band began as an instrumental group called the Tornadoes in 1961 in The Hague, Netherlands, with George Jan Kooymans (guitar), Rinus Gerritsen (bass and keyboards), Hans van Herwerden (guitar), and Freddie van der Hilst (drums). They changed their name in 1963 to Golden Earrings after the British instrumental group of the same name had a hit with "Telstar" in 1962. The new appellation was derived from a cabaret song in their repertoire originally sung by Marlene Dietrich in 1947, and then Peggy Lee, though in 1969 it was shortened to the singular. In 1964, it was decided that they would become a vocal group like the British Invasion "beat" bands coming out of England, and Frans Krassenburg was hired as their first lead singer. Other personnel changes would follow through 1970, after which the lineup with vocalist and multi-instrumentalist Barry Hay, drummer Cesar Zuiderwijk, and founding members Kooymans and Gerritsen would remain unchanged to the present.

From their 1965 debut recording of "Please Go" through 1968, the band released a number of pop rock singles and albums in the Netherlands with varying degrees of success. By 1969, however, the music of Golden Earring had begun to evolve to a harder form of rock. *Eight Miles High* contained an 18-minute cover version of the 1966 Byrds hit that could stretch to 45 minutes of psychedelia in concert. From 1969–84, they would make 13 trips to the U.S., opening for Rush, the Doobie Brothers, Santana, and .38 Special, while also appearing with Eric Clapton, Led Zeppelin, and Jimi Hendrix—who purportedly wanted Gerritsen for the Experience. Both Kooymans and Hay, the main songwriters, recorded solo projects, but being invited to open for the Who in 1972 on a European tour led to the solidifying of their progressive style and signing with Track Records. Following the release of "Radar Love" from *Moontan* in 1973, they actually had Kiss and Aerosmith opening for them. The single motored to #13, while the gold-selling album scored a notch higher.

The runaway success of "Radar Love" in the U.S. could not be sustained, unfortunately, though *Cut* in 1982 and the single "Twilight Zone" advanced to

The aggressive, progressive, and muscular riffs of George Kooymans belied the fey band name and album photo.

#24 and #10, respectively. "Twilight Zone" owed a good portion of its popularity to having one of the first accompanying rock videos on the emerging MTV. Ironically, a controversial video in 1984 for the international hit single "When the Lady Smiles" (featuring nudity and the rape of a nun) resulted in it being banned from MTV and bombing in the U.S., though Democratic presidential candidate Hillary Clinton used it unknowingly in her 2008 campaign. Following a tragic fire at Six Flags Great Adventure in 1984, the band retreated back to Europe to record and perform.

Amazingly, Golden Earring celebrated their 47th anniversary in 2008 and remain active with over 200 dates a year, even as all members have released solo albums. Their last studio production was crafted in 2003 when they recorded *Millbrook U.S.A.* in upstate New York, and they have a follow-up in the works along with planned shows in the UK in 2009 for the first time in 30 years. A possible return to the U.S. later in the year is also being bandied about.

How to Play It

In keeping with the hypnotic shuffle beat set up by drummer Cesar Zuiderwijk on his snare drum with the loosened snares and the propulsive and signature bass pattern of Rinus Gerritsen, guitarist George Kooymans swings like mad through the 52 epic measures of his syncopated, serpentine solo. Consisting of several movements like a rock symphony, it is an intelligent as well as a

viscerally stimulating example of post-sixties creativity.

For all practical purposes, Kooymans riffs over an implied one-chord vamp of F#m7. Significantly, besides engaging in the standard modal technique of creating musical tension and resolving to the root F# note, he also adds and inserts chordal forms, entering with triple stops in a repeating pattern through measures 1–4 that imply F#m, E, and D6 harmony over an F# bass vamp. Measures 5–8 function as a melodic "response" to the harmonic "call" of measures 1–4 with double stops in 6ths diatonic to the key of F#m. By measure 9, and through to measure 15, he has evolved to comping F#m and F#m7 chord forms at fret 2 as the "call" and answered with the "response" of bluesy licks in the root position of the F# minor pentatonic scale as presented in two four-measure patterns that are almost identical.

In measures 16–24, Kooymans cuts loose in the extension position of the F# minor pentatonic scale around fret 5. Taking full advantage of his whiny tone powered by a moderate amount of natural-sounding tube distortion, he improvises with bursts of notes dynamically placed among elastic bends. Observe that he also creates anticipation by emphasizing the E (♭7th) in measures 16, 17, 18, and 20, reserving resolution to the F# for the middle of the section in measures 19–20. In addition, the climactic descending run in measures 23–24 ends logically and with finality on the F# on string 6 at fret 2. A stunning break from the F# minor pentatonic scale, the speedy and flashy passage with multiple pull-offs includes a chromatic lick on strings 1 and 4, as well as the D# note on string 2 at fret 4 from the F# Dorian mode.

A dramatic, ascending, chromatic passage occurs in measures 25–30 as a *de facto*

interlude in the solo. Utilizing the root F# note as a pedal tone at fret 2 on string 6, Kooymans walks up from F# to A in measures 25–28 and then sustains a wonderfully dissonant B/F# double stop on strings 5 and 6 at fret 2 in measures 29–30. Combined with a synthesizer part, the effect is one of impending doom, in keeping with the dark lyric content of the song.

The final "movement" in measures 31–44 is somewhat of a reprise of the beginning featuring chords and chordal forms. Measures 33–35 employ octave F#m7 voicings combined with licks from the root-octave position of the F# minor pentatonic scale in syncopated rhythms. Kooymans then transitions to double stops implying the same tonality in "call and response" fashion for measures 36–39. He follows as the climax of his solo unfolds with a startling, siren-like harmony bend producing A#/F in measures 41–42 that is far outside the F#m tonality. A run down the root-octave position of the F# minor pentatonic scale with 4ths and 3rds in measure 43 over the C#5 change brings it back home by ending on the C# power chord of G#/C# in measure 44.

Vital Stats

Guitarist: George Kooymans

Song: "Radar Love"

Album: *Moontan –* Golden Earring

Age at time of recording: 25

Guitar: Ampeg Dan Armstrong Plexiglas guitar

Amp: Faylon

Track 14

2:49

Guitar Solo
Fast ♩ = 198

*F#m7

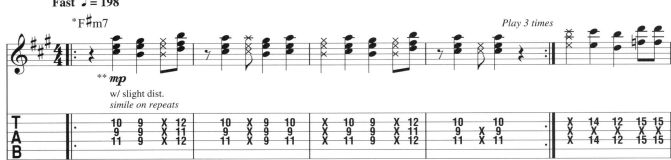

*Chord symbols reflect overall harmony.
**Played *mf* on repeats

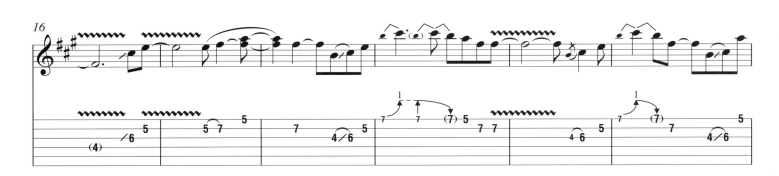

Words and Music by George Kooymans and Barry Hay
Copyright © 1973 Snamyook
Copyright Renewed
All Rights Administered by Sony/ATV Music Publishing, 8 Music Square West, Nashville, TN 37203
International Copyright Secured   All Rights Reserved

Joe Walsh

© Photofest

"Free gas for everyone."

—The campaign promise from Joe Walsh's unsuccessful presidential campaign in 1979

For a man known for his goofy sense of humor and interest in amply-endowed women, Joe Walsh has been a serious, focused guitar player for over four decades. His authentic blues chops, as well as his stylistic debt to the great British guitarists of the sixties, attest to his classic rock credibility.

Joseph Fidler Walsh was born on November 20, 1947, in Wichita, Kansas. He played the oboe and clarinet as a child and the bass as a teenager with the G-Clefs and Nomads. While attending Kent State University in Ohio from 1965–69, he played guitar in the Measles until drummer Jim Fox and bassist Tom Kriss hired him as lead singer and guitarist in their Cleveland power trio, the James Gang. *Y'er Album* was released in 1969, followed by the great *Rides Again* in 1970 at #20, which featured the classic "Funk #49." Pete Townshend acknowledged Walsh by inviting the James Gang to open for the Who on a European tour, and he also appeared with B.B. King on *Indianola Mississippi Seeds*. The aptly named *Thirds* appeared in 1971, and likewise made fans at #27, sporting "Walk Away" (#51), but Walsh "walked away" from the band after the release of their *Live in Concert* album.

He moved to Colorado in 1972 and formed Barnstorm with bassist Kenny Passarelli and drummer Joe Vitale and released a self-titled debut album. It eased into the Top 100 at #79 and contained the first version of his dramatic "Turn to Stone." *The Smoker You Drink, the Player You Get* (1973) exposed his wit and wide musical vision, and he was rewarded with #6 for the album and #23 for the heavy blues boogie of "Rocky Mountain Way." Tragically, his young daughter Emma was killed in a car accident in 1974, contributing to his eventual alcohol problem.

Walsh relocated to L.A. for *So What* (#11) that reflected his state of mind in 1974. Following the live *You Can't Argue with a Sick Mind* (#20) in 1976, Walsh replaced Bernie Leadon in the Eagles. It was a fortuitous move for him and the band as he added a major jolt of blues rock guitar firepower and songwriting (particularly with "Life in the Fast Lane") to their epochal #1 monster hit and Grammy-winning *Hotel California*.

The "player you get" is one of the best, a phenomenal blues rocker with just enough humor to avoid pretentiousness.

Walsh then split his winners between the Eagles and his solo career. The former released two more albums before their infamous breakup in 1980. Meanwhile, in 1978 Walsh released *But Seriously, Folks...* as his commercial high point (#8) with the wryly autobiographical "Life's Been Good" (#12). *There Goes the Neighborhood* (1981) was also a hit (#20), but it signaled a gradual tapering off in quality with his last Top 40 hit "Life of Illusion" as his drinking problem escalated. In 1989 and 1992, he toured with Ringo Starr's All-Starr Band. The Eagles, including Walsh, reunited in 1994 for an MTV special, *Hell Freezes Over*, and subsequent tours with the stipulation he stay sober. In 1998, the band was inducted into the Rock and Roll Hall of Fame and in 2007 released the #1 charting *Long Road Out of Eden*.

Though he released his last solo album, *Song for a Dying Planet*, to little interest in 1992, Walsh has been busy. He received an honorary doctorate from Kent State University in 2001, gave a kicking performance at Eric Clapton's Crossroads Guitar Festival in 2004, and even indulged in a brief, satisfying reunion with the James Gang in 2006. The following year, he embarked on a short solo tour and remains alive and kicking.

How to Play It

The seventies were a distant time when a stone slow country blues groove with slide guitar in open E tuning could become a Top 40 radio hit. Of course, the boogie shuffle beat is timeless, and few, if any, singles containing it—from the Eagles' "Heartache Tonight" to Melissa Etheridge's "I'm the Only One"—have failed to chart over the years.

Following his trendy "talk box" solo (not shown) that vamps hard on the E chord, Walsh bottlenecks back in with a flaming slide solo to the fade in measure 24. Measures 1–8 contain the same boogie patterns along with A5 and E5 chords as in the chorus (not shown) for an uplift effect resulting from starting on the IV (A) chord instead of the E (I). Be aware that, in open E, the open strings and all the notes at fret 12 consist of the E (root), G♯ (3rd), and B (5th) notes from an E major triad. The notes at fret 5 and fret 17 are the A (root), C♯ (3rd), and E (5th) from an A major triad. Likewise, the notes at fret 7 or fret 19 are B (root), D♯ (3rd), and F♯ (5th) from a B major triad. In other words, it is possible to easily follow the three chord changes of a blues progression by relocating the slider to the appropriate fret position and playing the same pattern. In open-tuned slide, it is standard operating procedure to follow blues chord changes by changing scales instead of improvising "modally" in the key of the song.

Following protocol, Walsh settles in at fret 17 for measures 1–2 over the A change and wiggles around most prominently on strings 1–3 where the root, 5th, and 3rd notes lie conveniently. However, in measures 3–4 over the E chord, rather than switching to fret 12, he chooses to move outside the major harmony and adds the tension-inducing tones of G and A from the E minor pentatonic scale, along with resolution to the root note on beat 1 of measure 4. In measures 5–6 over the A chord, Walsh builds interest by moving from fret 17, where he works the C♯ and E notes, to measure 10, where the G and A notes impart an A7 tonality and the A note on string 2 sets up the move to the root B note at fret 12 in measure 7 of the B change. Anticipating the return to E beginning in measure 9, Walsh builds exciting musical tension with phrasing and note selection by repeating the blues-approved D (♭3rd) in conjunction with the root in measure 8.

Measures 9–24 contain the signature two-measure vamp of D5 and the E boogie pattern from the interlude (not shown), that in itself creates tension and resolution. Walsh continues alternating on the D and B notes in measures 9 and 10 to cruise into the concluding section of his slide solo. In addition, observe how he plays "in between" micro-tones in measures 10 and 11 notated in tab as "14.5" and "11.5," respectively, as a way to achieve special bluesy tension. Through measure 15, he keeps the pot on boil with bluesy dissonance and steady resolution to the root E note. However, starting in measure 16, he engages in "call and response" with himself by playing roaring D and E chords on the bass strings and answering with short, tart retorts in E around fret 12.

Vital Stats

Guitarist: Joe Walsh

Song: "Rocky Mountain Way"

Album: *The Smoker You Drink, the Player You Get*

Age at time of recording: 26

Guitar: Gibson Les Paul Goldtop

Amp: Pre-CBS Fender Super Reverb

Words and Music by Joe Walsh, Joe Vitale, Ken Passarelli and Rocke Grace
Copyright © 1973 SONGS OF UNIVERSAL, INC., BARNSTORM MUSIC and BELKIN MUSIC COMPANY
Copyright Renewed
All Rights Controlled and Administered by SONGS OF UNIVERSAL, INC.
All Rights Reserved   Used by Permission

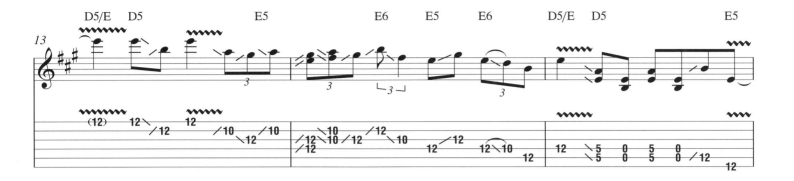

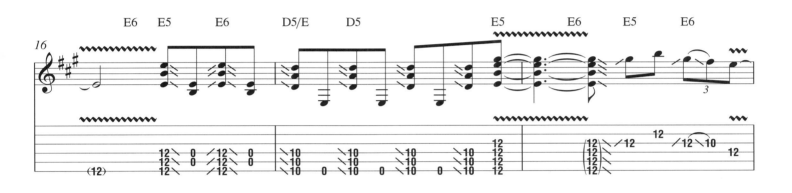

Begin fade

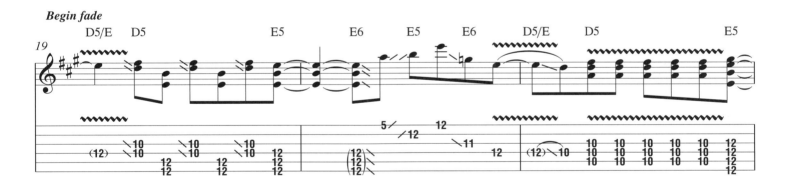

Fade out

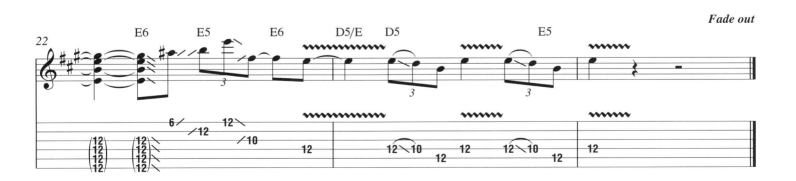

Rick Derringer

"I'm still learning about the guitar… and life."

—Rick Derringer

Rick Derringer enjoys the distinction of heading one of the few American blues-based bands to briefly hold the line against the oncoming British Invasion. As the lead singer and guitarist of the McCoys, he played a stinging solo on their #1 hit "Hang on Sloopy" (1965) and then went on to play with and produce a wide range of famous artists as well as enjoying an ongoing solo career.

Derringer was born Richard Zehringer on August 5, 1947, in Celina, Ohio. With his younger brother Randy on drums, bassist Randy Jo Hobbs, saxophonist Sean Michaels, and key-boardist Ronnie Brandon, they went from Rick and the Raiders to the McCoys in 1965. Rick eventually changed his name to "Derringer" after seeing a Derringer pistol pictured on the Bang Records label. The band moved to New York City but never duplicated the success of "Hang on Sloopy" (the official state song of Ohio), gamely evolving away from their "bubblegum" recordings to become a psychedelic rock band in the late sixties.

In 1970, Derringer, Randy, and bassist Hobbs backed Johnny Winter to become the raunchy blues-rocking Johnny Winter Band. The debut album featured Derringer's production, guitar, and "Rock and Roll Hoochie Koo" that he penned especially for Winter. Derringer also played on and produced *Edgar Winter's White Trash* (1971) and the live, two-disc *Roadwork* from 1972 that became a mega-hit.

In 1973, he released *All American Boy*. An appealing combination of teeny-bopper rock, blues rock, and pop rock, it went to #25, while his classic version of "Rock and Roll Hoochie Koo" hit #23. Though an impressive debut, he was not yet ready to make a go of it alone and continued producing records for the Winter brothers. Finally, in 1975, he assembled "Derringer" with guitarist Danny Johnson, bassist Kenny Aaronson, and drummer Vinny Appice and headed out gigging to cheers, opening for Aerosmith and Led Zeppelin, among others. Following the release of the disappointing *Springtime* with the fey cover photo the same year, Derringer had his road band back him on the cleverly named *Derringer* in 1976 and *Sweet Evil* in 1977.

His band deserted him in 1978, and a downturn began in Derringer's recording

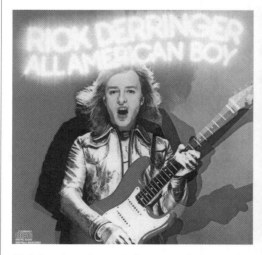

Rick Derringer's magic fingers probably could play right through the silver lamé gloves!

career. There were exceptions like *Guitars and Women* produced by Todd Rundgren in 1979, however, and his excellent soloing is almost always in evidence. He went on to employ his extensive experience as a producer and guitarist for artists as varied as Meatloaf, Bette Midler, Kiss, Barbra Streisand, and Alice Cooper. In addition, he toured with Cyndi Lauper for six years as her guitarist and five years with "Weird Al" Yankovic. Derringer won a Grammy in 1984 along with Yankovic for Best Comedy Album, *"Weird Al" Yankovic in 3-D*, on which he imitated Eddie Van Halen on the Michael Jackson parody, "Eat It."

Back to the Blues (1993), *Electra Blues* (1994), *Blues Deluxe* (1998), and *Jackhammer Blues* (2000) provided unencumbered opportunities for him to wail, and he also took an unsuccessful stab at jazz with the mostly instrumental *Free Ride* in 2002. By 2004, he and his wife Brenda were producing Christian rock records featuring their children, and Derringer has since changed the lyrics to some of his old hits to reflect his religious beliefs. In 2008, he and Edgar Winter jammed with Johnny Winter for the first time in many years.

How to Play It

Rick Derringer has been cited by BMI for his signature song having amassed over one million airplays. No doubt more than a few of those plays inspired young pickers to take a shot at learning his scorching, sixteenth-note laden solo or, at the very least, acquire a healthy dose of his rambunctious energy and totally

aggressive string attack. As he declaims in the vocal, "Yeah, somebody said 'Keep on rockin'."

Derringer jumps right into measures 1–8 of his 16-measure solo and blazes with an intensity rarely seen even in the greatest classic rock. Using the one-measure vamp of A5–C5–D5–C5 as his harmonic base, he rips hot licks in the roo-octave position of the A minor pentatonic scale. The blues is his muse, and he strings together (pun intended!) riff after riff from his vast repertoire. Measures 1 and 3 contain a screaming harmony bend motif that is a favorite of heavy blues-rockers who want a quick shot of musical tension. As is the custom, Derringer then runs down the scale in measures 2 and 4 with resolution to the root A note on string 4 at fret 19. Measures 5 and 6 continue with a similar approach: Derringer creates tension in the former with a "Blues 101" lick on beat 1 involving a whole-step bend to E (5th) on string 3 at fret 19 followed by the E and A notes on strings 2 and 1 at fret 17, while releasing it at the latter with a blur of descending notes. In measures 8 and 9, however, he opts to maintain focus on the root note while continually alternating with the defining blues tone, C ($\flat$3rd), either singly or in combination with the E for the tangy E/C dyad.

Measures 9–16 function as a *de facto* "part 2" of the solo as Derringer takes a completely different tack by dramatically dropping down to the root position of the A minor pentatonic scale at fret 5. The move also provides welcome contrast from the unrelenting high-register onslaught experienced in measures 1–8. Along with the change of

"venue," Derringer reverses his approach by starting with resolution to the A note in measures 9 and 11 and making musical tension in the alternate measures of 10 and 12. Observe that the harmony bends in measure 10 echo those in measures 1 and 3 but are an octave lower and extend the motif. In measures 13 and 14, Derringer anticipates the climax of his solo in measures 15–16 by cranking up the tension in both measures. Check out how the unison bends to the blues-approved C in measure 13 at fret 13 produce the desired result and offer dynamic contrast to the roaring ascending run in measure 14 that continues unabated in measure 15 as Derringer flies up through the extension position of the scale, ending at fret 10. In measure 16, he reverses course to wisely turn down the heat before running out of his allotted space (at least via the register), though he still refuses to cut back on the sizzling sixteenth-notes with which he singes his strings until the very end.

Vital Stats

Guitarist: Rick Derringer

Song: "Rock and Roll Hoochie Koo"

Album: *All American Boy*

Age at time of recording: 25

Guitar: 1959 Fender Stratocaster with Gibson stop tailpiece given to him by Johnny Winter—purportedly the Strat Dylan used to "go electric"

Amp: Marshall

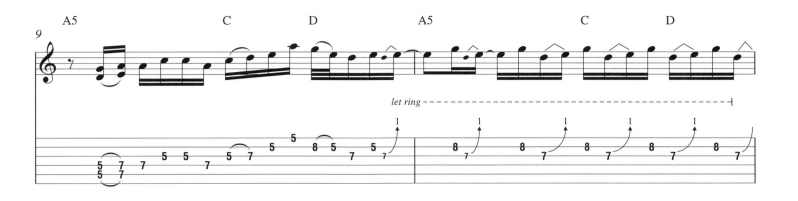

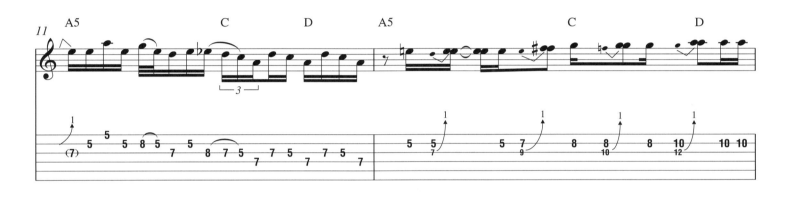

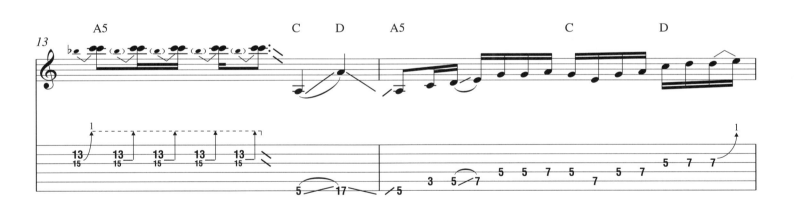

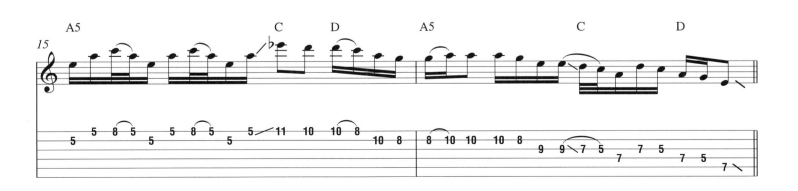

Ed King

Led by their brawling lead singer Ronnie Van Zant, Lynyrd Skynyrd created sinewy blues rock crunch with intelligent

"I am mainly known as the one who verbally counted off 'Sweet Home Alabama...' "

—Ed King

and knowing lyrics. Along with the Allman Brothers, and to a lesser degree the Marshall Tucker Band, they kicked southern rock into the mainstream in the seventies before MTV in the eighties spelled the death knell for long-haired, southern "good ole boys."

In 1964, Gary Rossington and fellow guitarist Allen Collins, Van Zant, drummer Bob Burns, and bassist Larry Jungstrom decided to form a band in Jacksonville, Florida. Their memorable name came from Leonard Skinner, a dictatorial gym teacher who stated the boys "would never amount to anything good in life." Van Zant suggested the name, and bassist Jungstrom was replaced by Leon Wilkerson while keyboardist Billy Powell was added. By 1969, they had a following in north Florida and Georgia, and a year later, famed musician/producer Al Kooper heard them in Atlanta and signed them to his Sounds of the South label. Guitarist Ed King, formerly of Strawberry Alarm Clock, was brought in as yet a third hot picker. *Pronounced Leh-nerd Skin-nerd* (#27) was released in 1973 and, coupled with their opening act slot on the Who's Quadrophenia tour and the radio exposure granted "Free Bird," Lynyrd Skynyrd broke out as raw-edged musical rebels.

Second Helping (#12) in 1974 proved more successful, as the single "Sweet Home Alabama" (#12) would become the band's top hit. *Nuthin' Fancy* (#9) with "Saturday Night Special" (#27) was completed in bits and pieces in the midst of gigging during 1975. Burns was replaced by Artimus Pyle, and guitarist King opted out due to stress. *Gimme Back My Bullets* (#20) followed in 1976. Looking to gas up their guitar lineup again, 26-year-old Steve Gaines was added for the double live *One More from the Road* (#9) featuring "Free Bird" (#19), and the band toured the UK with the Stones.

Street Survivors (#5) in 1977 recaptured their initial energy while also reflecting a new maturity. On October 20, however, Lynyrd Skynyrd's chartered airplane dropped out of the sky on the way to a gig in Baton Rouge, Louisiana, and crashed in a Mississippi swamp. Van Zant, Steve, his sister Cassie Gaines, and road manager Dean Kilpatrick were killed, while the remainder of the group and crew were seriously injured. The

The "homey" title was ironic given the crunching, British rock by-way-of-Dixie music impatiently waiting inside to jump out and slap the listener upside the head.

devastation of the tragedy was so enormous that Rossington and Collins decided not to continue as Lynyrd Skynyrd. By 1980, however, they were sufficiently recovered to form the Rossington-Collins Band with Leon Wilkerson and Billy Powell. Recruiting female singer Dale Krantz (whom Rossington eventually married) as front-person, they recorded the gold *Anytime, Anyplace, Anywhere* (#13) in 1980 and *This Is the Way* (#24) in 1982. In 1983, Collins went solo, but tragedy struck again when he was left paralyzed following a car accident in 1986.

A reunion tour commenced in 1987 with surviving Skynyrd members recording *Southern by the Grace of God: Lynyrd Skynyrd Tribute Tour, Vol. 1* (#68) in 1988. Allen Collins died of respiratory failure in 1990 even as the surviving members would be made honorary colonels in the Alabama State Militia for "Sweet Home Alabama." Sadly, in 2001, Leon Wilkerson died of cirrhosis of the liver, adding to the growing list of casualties. Against all odds, however, Gary Rossington led a version of Lynyrd Skynyrd with a club gig in Manhattan in the summer of 2004 for the Republican National Convention, though Ed King was unable to tour due to heart problems. In 2006, Skynyrd was inducted into the Rock and Roll Hall of Fame, and on January 28, 2009, yet another member fell when Billy Powell died of a heart attack.

How to Play It

Ed King claims that his iconic solo in the most iconic of southern rock classics came to him completely arranged in a dream. Whatever the derivation of his inspiration, it is a masterpiece of taste, tone, and technique and one of a select group of solos that many guitarists could sing note for note from memory.

The 16-measure progression in G is composed of the two-measure vamp from the verses (not shown) containing D–C–G changes repeated eight times. The "secret" to King's successful soloing strategy is his use of the G major pentatonic scale voiced as the E minor pentatonic scale in several positions. A popular option for many blues, blues rock, and country guitarists, the minor pentatonic fingerings are especially friendly for sweet major pentatonic bends, in addition to pull-offs and hammer-ons, and was primarily developed by B.B. King in the late fifties.

Being that the chords go by quickly, King does not follow the changes per se, but instead phrases modally with an unerring sense of swing and drive. He builds waves of musical tension, both melodic and otherwise, with only occasional well-placed resolution to the root G note occurring after using it prominently in measure 2 to initially establish the tonality. Along those lines, the highlight of the solo occurs in measures 9 and 10 where King repeatedly bangs on and vibratos the G on string 1 at fret 15. Simple as the concept is, the effect is cathartic and intensified due to the blistering, repeating patterns in the root-octave position of the E *hexatonic* (a variation on the minor pentatonic) scale in the preceding measures of 5–7 that set up the dynamics. Check out how, during the repeating riffs, he pulls off from the C at fret 17 on string 3 to the root G note at fret 12, a highly unusual and striking move in rock music. Following is the rollicking run up the root-octave position of the E minor pentatonic scale in measure 8 that resolves to the stinging G notes in measure 9.

Along the way, King does favor a few other choice notes, however, such as the B bent up from the A, functioning as the smooth major 7th over the C chord in measures 1, 3, and 15. Another example is the E that naturally falls under the fingers in the root-octave position of the E minor pentatonic scale as seen in measures 5–8 and 11. As the 2nd of D, major tonality-defining 3rd of C, and sweet 6th of G, the E harmonizes with all three chords.

In measures 12–16, King rolls fluidly down and up the E minor pentatonic scale with steady sixteenth notes at frets 10, 12, and in the extension position above the root-octave position. The unstoppable forward momentum is a bracing counterpoint to the rocky rhythm, and the dynamics of long runs in the treble and bass registers serve as an intense audio rush during the conclusion of the solo. With logic and finality, King ends on the root G note on beat 4 of measure 16.

Vital Stats

Guitarist: Ed King

Song: "Sweet Home Alabama"

Album: *Second Helping* – Lynyrd Skynyrd

Age at time of recording: 25

Guitar: 1973 Fender Strat

Amp: Prototype Peavey Roadmaster

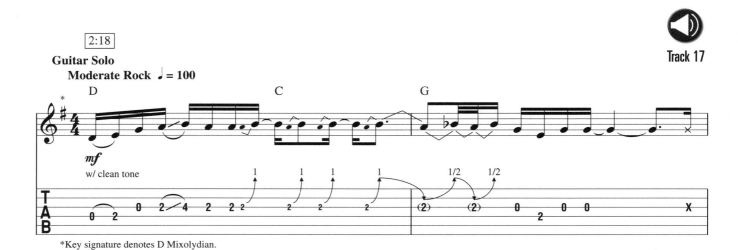

*Key signature denotes D Mixolydian.

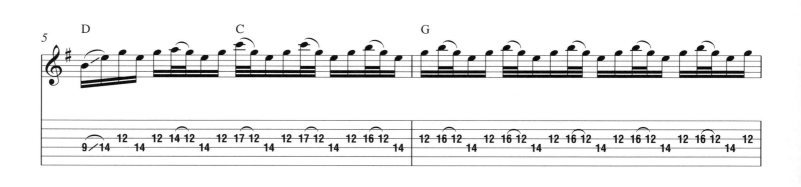

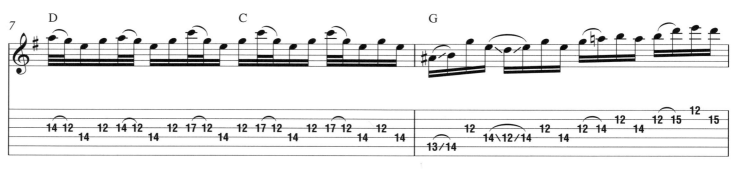

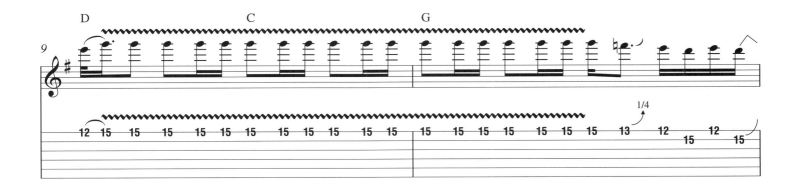

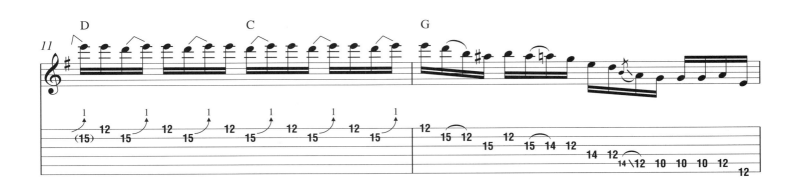

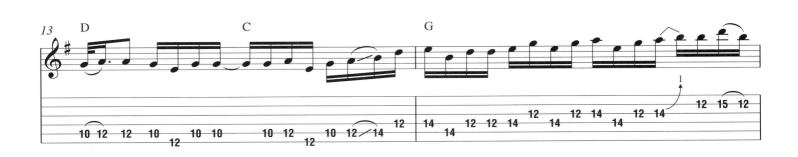

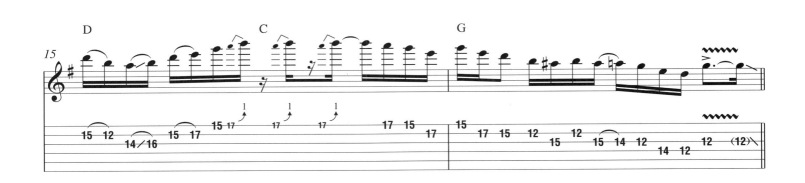

Steve Hunter

Courtesy of Steve Hunter

"Sex, drugs, and rock 'n' roll... take out the drugs and you've got more time for the other two."

—Steven Tyler

Seminal British Invasion blues bands like the Yardbirds and the Rolling Stones inspired American bands to pursue their own dreams of original blues rock. One of the best and most successful has been Aerosmith from Boston— that bastion of American colonial resistance.

In 1969, vocalist and drummer Steven Tyler (née Tallorico) from Yonkers, N.Y., was blown away by guitarist Joe Perry and bassist Tom Hamilton playing in Jam Band in Sunapee, New Hampshire. They eventually formed a power trio before adding second guitarist Roy Tabano and drummer Joey Kramer. It was Kramer who suggested the name "Aerosmith" after being inspired by *Aerial Ballet* by Harry Nilson. In 1971, they moved to Boston where Tabano was replaced by Brad Whitford.

Aerosmith caught their break in 1972 at Max's Kansas City in NYC where Clive Davis from Columbia heard them. Their self-titled debut (#21 when re-released in 1976) appeared in 1973 with "Dream On" (#59, but #6 when re-released in 1976). A period of intense touring sharpened them up for *Get Your Wings* (#74) in 1974, highlighted by the steaming "Train Kept A-Rollin'." The masterful *Toys in the Attic* (#11) the following year confirmed their arrival with "Sweet Emotion" (#36), "Walk This Way" (#10), and the title track. *Rocks* (#3) in 1976 solidified Aerosmith's rock-hard reputation and went platinum.

The hits kept coming with *Draw the Line* (#11) in 1977, *Live! Bootleg* (#13) in 1978, and *Night in the Ruts* (#14) in 1979, but the rampant drug use, especially by Tyler and Perry, roiled the band. Perry quit to go solo, and Whitford followed in 1980. Guitarists Jimmy Crespo and Rick Dufay were brought in and did a credible job on *Rock in a Hard Place* (#32) in 1982. In 1984, Perry and Whitford returned for the Back in the Saddle tour, and Aerosmith released *Done with Mirrors* (#36) in 1985 to inaugurate what would be a stunning comeback. Tyler and Perry entered rehab, and in 1986 appeared on Run-D.M.C.'s smash hip hop version of "Walk This Way," which also commenced Aerosmith's ascendance as MTV icons.

Permanent Vacation (#11) with "Dude (Looks Like a Lady)" (#14), the title track (#11), "Angel" (#3), and "Rag Doll" (#17) in 1987, benefited greatly from a new producer and hip outside songwriters, reviving a band considered burnt-out. *Pump* (#5), two years later, confirmed that Aerosmith was back, baby, with the power and swagger of old, while winning a Grammy for "Janie's

The "bad boys from Boston" had more in common with the Yardbirds than they realized when Steve Hunter and Dick Wagner were brought in as ringers for "Train Kept A-Rollin'." Almost ten years earlier, Jeff Beck had surreptitiously recorded tracks with the British Invasion blues rockers while Clapton "fiddled."

Got a Gun" (#4). Massachusetts Governor William Weld declared April 13, 1993, "Aerosmith Day," and *Get a Grip* (#3) the same year hewed to the winning formula and scored a Grammy for "Livin' on the Edge."

In 1997, the much-ballyhooed *Nine Lives* (#1) with the #1 title track was released. Band tensions arose again during the recording process, but a Grammy was awarded for "Pink" (#27). The live and ironic *A Little South of Sanity* (#6) with the hit title track (#12) followed in 1998. It would be three years before *Just Push Play* (#2) with a #2 title track and "Jaded" (#7) signaled yet another "comeback" as they played the 2001 Super Bowl and were inducted into the Rock and Roll Hall of Fame. In 2004, Aerosmith put out their first "blues" album with *Honkin' on Bobo* (#5). In 2006, Tyler underwent successful throat surgery, and in 2008, *Guitar Hero: Aerosmith* was released. Joe Perry underwent successful knee surgery in January 2009 resulting from an onstage fall years earlier.

How to Play It

By now it is a well-known "secret" that session legends Steve Hunter and Dick Wagner performed the blistering solos on "Train Kept A-Rollin'," as opposed to Aerosmith lead guitarist Joe Perry. Hunter plays the third solo with swooping, lyrical lines following verse 2 (not shown). A veteran of stints with Mitch Ryder and Alice Cooper who in later years famously backed Lou Reed,

he is a true unsung rock guitar hero on par with any of his more esteemed peers.

The 21-measure solo consists of an altered arrangement of I, IV, and V chord changes after verse 2. Brad Whitford first establishes a foundation with a creative, funky walking bass-string pattern in E in unison with bassist Tom Hamilton in measures 1–4 that is not on the Yardbirds version. Following a time-warping, double-string bend of F♯/D as he enters the fray on beat 1 of measure 5 over the A5 (IV) change, Hunter parks in the root and extension positions of the A composite blues scale (Mixolydian mode plus blues scale) through measure 9. Note how he blasts right off playing astoundingly fast, fluid, and clean sixteenth-note licks that glide effortlessly over beats and bar lines in striking rhythmic contrast to the highly syncopated bass line.

In measures 9–12 over the E change, Hunter smoothly and smartly switches to the E minor pentatonic scale starting at fret 9 and powers up to the root-octave position in measure 11 for a climactic buildup leading to the critical B5 (V) chord in measure 13. As the band dramatically and dynamically rests, Hunter "sings out" with classic blues bends and licks as a prelude to the exuberant chromatic walkup from B5–F♯5 that occurs in measure 14 where he unleashes an astonishing blur of notes. The stunning transition leads to the G change and measures 15–21 that resort back to the classic, chunky rhythm pattern identified with "Train Kept A-Rollin'," though performed at half-time tempo compared to the Yardbirds. Hunter, however, does not back off for a moment. In measures 15–18, he "slices

and dices" the root and extension positions of the E minor pentatonic scale like a Samurai guitarist, bending, pulling off, and vibratoing with surgical precision. Of special interest is his addition of the G♯ note at fret 16 in measure 17 over the A chord that, because of the half step between G♯ and A, contributes an element of melody not easily produced in the pentatonic scale, as well as intensifying forward movement to resolution on the root A note.

As he did in measure 14, Hunter delivers a crushing salvo in measure 18 over the G5 chord with sextuplets in the root and extension positions of the E minor pentatonic scale that swivels and swings. The dynamic roller coaster chord sequence of A5–B5–A5–G5–F♯5 in measure 19 finds him literally taking his solo to a new level in the same scale around fret 20 where his proletariat Les Paul TV model flies and screams like an eagle. With the A bent up one step to B over the B change, followed by the D bent up one step to E in measures 20–21 over the G chord, Hunter sets the bar high for aggressive blues rock rarely equaled and never surpassed.

Vital Stats

Guitarist: Steve "The Deacon" Hunter

Song: "Train Kept A-Rollin'"

Album: *Get Your Wings* – Aerosmith

Age at time of recording: 24

Guitar: 1959 Les Paul TV model w/ single P-90 pickup

Amp: 1950s tweed Fender Twin

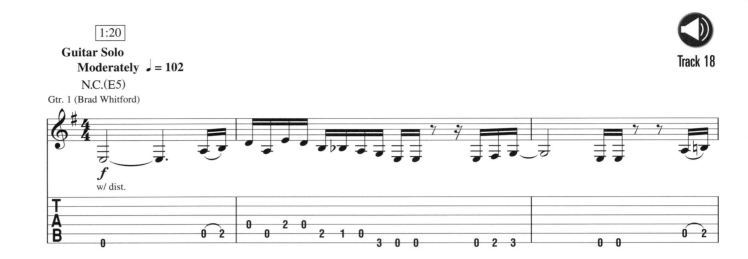

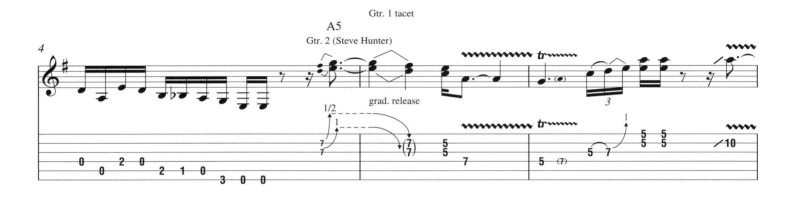

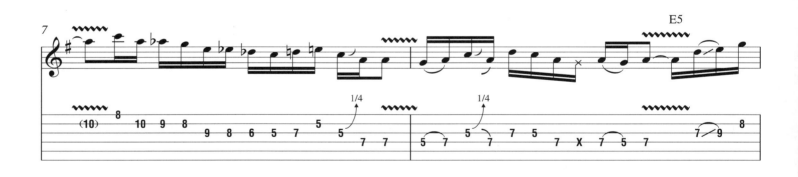

Words and Music by Tiny Bradshaw, Lois Mann and Howie Kay

Billy Gibbons

Sexual innuendo has been an element of rock music from the beginning, as the term itself is a euphemism. However, ZZ Top may have pulled off the biggest goof of all on the public airwaves when they titled their lascivious shuffle blues with a Yiddish expression for "buttocks."

In 1969, William "Rev. Willie G." Gibbons from the Moving Sidewalks and bassist Dusty Hill and drummer Frank Beard from American Blues formed ZZ Top down the Houston, Texas, way with assistance of manager Bill Ham. ZZ

Top's First Album of primal electric blues came out well under the radar in 1970. *Rio Grande Mud* (#109) in 1972 with the chugging "Francine" (#69), however, displayed Gibbons' developing gift for composing catchy, riff-driven, original blues rock with wit and low-down raunch. The highlight of their "blue period" would be the gold *Tres Hombres* (#8) in 1974 sporting the classic John Lee Hooker tribute, "La Grange" (#41). The "Little Ol' Band from Texas" had found the formula that would serve them through *Fandango* (#10 in 1975) featuring "Tush" (#20), *Tejas* (#17 in 1976) with "It's Only Love" (#44), and *Deguello* (#24 in 1979) containing "Cheap Sunglasses" (#89) and the Sam & Dave cover, "I Thank You" (#34).

El Loco (#17) in 1981 with "Leila" (#77) was a transition to the extremely slick, streamlined disco-boogie that followed and brought ZZ Top unimagined success. As a tribute to their roots, however, the band took a plank of wood from the cabin Muddy Waters was born in and had it made into the "Muddywood" guitar, which was sent on a tour to raise money for the Delta Blues Museum. *Eliminator* (#9) in 1983 may have been a cynical ploy to capitalize on MTV and the synth and sequenced eighties, but it worked big time. "Gimme All Your Lovin'" (#37), "Sharp Dressed Man" (#56), and "Legs" (#8) made the trio video heroes with sexy hot rods, sexy girls, and long beards (except for Frank Beard!). *Afterburner* (#4) in 1985 was more of the same and

"Lightnin' Hopkins taught us that, 'The rubber on the wheel is faster than the rubber on the heel,' and Muddy Waters taught us, 'You don't have to be the best one, just be a good 'un'... that just about says it all: Always strive to be a good 'un."
—Billy Gibbons

even more popular with "Sleeping Bag" (#8), "Rough Boy" (#22), "Stages" (#21), and "Velcro Fly" (#35). Five long years later, *Recycler* (#6 in 1990) completed the platinum trilogy

With a live side and a studio side, the tres hombres neatly encapsulated their early years of rocking out hot, blue, and righteous.

with "Give It Up" (#79), but it was clearly time for a change, despite the heady sales.

After a three-year layoff, the Top returned with *Antenna* (#14) in 1994 that was over-enthusiastically touted as a return to the glory days of *Tres Hombres*. Better was a compilation of their original blues compositions called *One Foot in the Blues* the same year. *Rhythmeen* (#29), which translates to "mean rhythm," in 1996 was a better effort that finally laid the synthesized eighties to rest with its bold guitars. In 1997, ZZ Top performed at Superbowl XXXI.

XXX (#100) in 1999, celebrating their record 30th anniversary, should have been an unabashed triumph, but like their previous recent records, it lacked the deep blues grooves of their early seventies masterpieces. *Mescalero* (#57) was an encouraging improvement in 2003 as the band appeared to be struggling mightily to find their way back to the blues as they once played it with unquestioned authenticity and sly humor. In 2004, ZZ Top was inducted into the Rock and Roll Hall of Fame, and in the fall of 2008, it was announced they would be recording a new album with famed, ubiquitous producer Rick Rubin and the Black Keys.

How to Play It

The right good "Rev. Gibbons" preaches the gospel of the blues with a slashing slide solo in two thumping 12-bar choruses. Remarkable if it had appeared on a true blues album, it was thrilling to hear on Top 40 radio in 1975, and it inspired more than a few rock guitarists to expand their techniques beyond conventional lead guitar playing.

Just as remarkable, Gibbons performs in standard tuning with such advanced skill and clarity that his solo could be mistaken for being in the more harmonious and advantageous open G tuning. His "secret" is playing fat slide harmonies in standard tuning. The G (I), C (IV), and D (V) major triads lay on strings 2, 3, and 4 at the twelfth, fifth, and seventh positions, respectively. Hence, Gibbons follows the changes of the blues progression by relocating his slider to each appropriate fret position as opposed to just fooling around in the G minor pentatonic scale, for example.

In measures 1–4 of the first chorus, he whomps down hard on the root G note on string 3 at fret 12 while ladling in the D note on string 4 and the B on string 2. Observe the tasty addition of the C (♭7th) at fret 10 that produces a little bluesy tang and anticipates the C chords in measures 5–6. After defining the C change at fret 5, Gibbons follows logically with G7 (fret 12) in measures 7–8, D7 (fret 7) in measure 9, C7 (fret 5) in measure 10, G7 (fret 12) in measure 11, and a bluesy dissonance in measure 12 over D with the F (♭3rd) note. Check out the two pull-offs of B♭ to the twangy open G string on beat 4 of measure 7 that are played with a grab by the left-hand index finger, instead of the slider, for variety and to draw extra attention to the G tonality.

With little deviation in concept, Gibbons basically repeats his soloing strategy in measures 13–24 for the second 12-bar chorus. Nonetheless, he does embellish his chord positions with notes from the G minor pentatonic scale that reside in close proximity to the triads. The most prominent and important occurs beginning in measure 19 over the G7 chord where he utilizes the B♭ (♭3rd) at fret 11 and the F (♭7th) at fret 10 "blue notes" to create musical tension that is resolved on the root G notes in measure 20. The highlight, however, follows in measure 21 over the crucial D7 change where Gibbons runs up to the root and extension positions of the scale for a dynamic and intense climax. Keeping the tension wicked up to a maximum, he descends in the extension position in measure 22 over the C7 chord, only briefly touching on the root C note, while playing a lick on beat 4 that anticipates the G change coming up in measure 23 by implying G and G9 harmonies. After conclusively resolving to the G7 chord in measure 23 with the same double stops, Gibbons additionally goes outside the basic harmony with a short run up the G major scale that ends on the A note functioning as the 5th in order to maintain some momentum into verse 3 (not shown).

Vital Stats

Guitarist: Billy Gibbons

Song: "Tush"

Album: *Fandango* – ZZ Top

Age at time of recording: 25

Guitar: 1959 sunburst Gibson Les Paul Standard, dubbed "Pearly Gates"

Amp: Early sixties brown Fender Deluxe

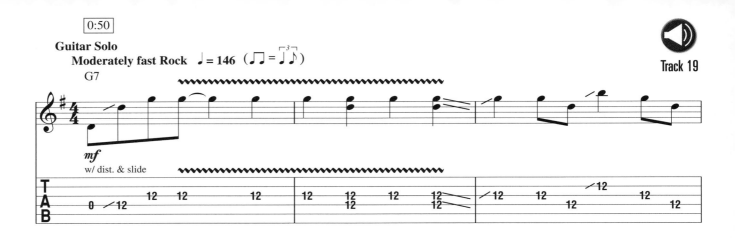

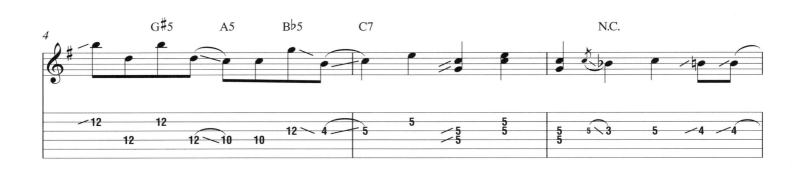

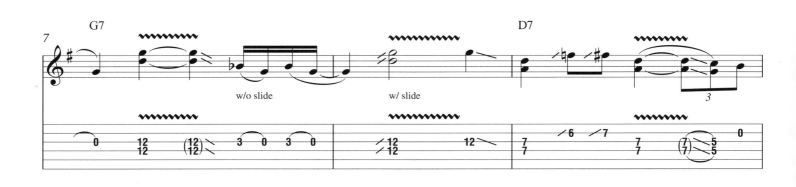

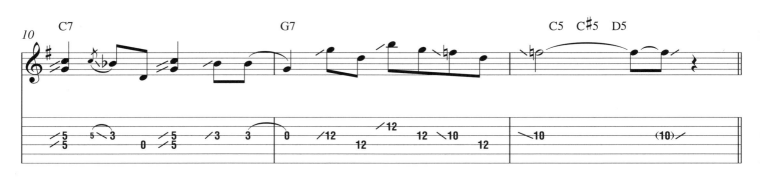

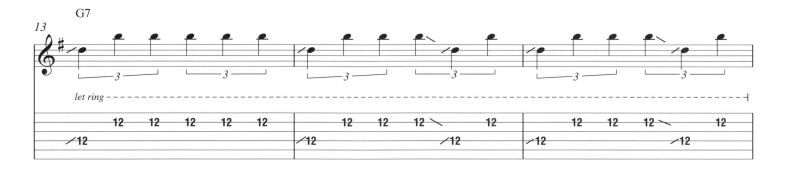

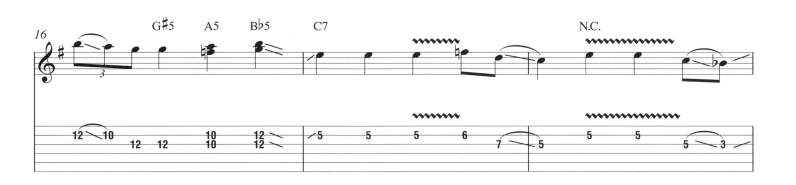

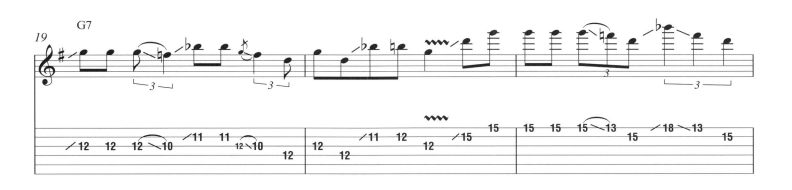

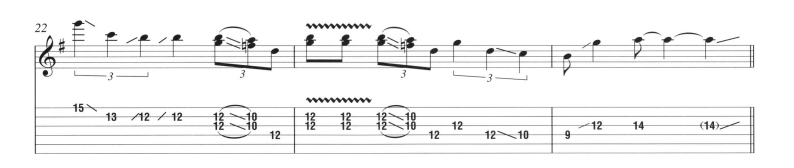

Tom Scholz

As has happened on several momentous occasions throughout rock history, a band bucked the prevailing trends of the era with crunch chords and extended, improvised solos. Boston, named for the historic city on the brackish Back Bay in Massachusetts, was rewarded in 1976 for their tenacity with one of the fastest-selling debut albums in pop music history. *Boston* went gold in two months, platinum in three months, and 17 times platinum by 2003. In the process, it contributed to reviving FM rock radio in the late seventies.

The road to immortality for Boston was anything but typical. Lead guitarist, chief songwriter, and CEO Donald Thomas "Tom" Scholz was a 1970 MIT graduate with a master's degree in mechanical engineering who went to work for Polaroid. After becoming disillusioned in the early seventies with a jam band containing singer Brad Delp and guitarist Barry Goudreau, he began realizing his dream of rock glory by creating demos in his 12-track basement studio. Scholz had been a fan of Cream and other heavy blues rock groups of the sixties, as well as the layered harmony guitars of Todd Rundgren, and set about creating an album of perfectly crafted songs on which he played most of the guitar, bass, and keyboard parts with Delp singing lead. The demos reached Epic Records in 1975, resulting in a contract, though an accommodation was reached where

some material had to be recorded in a "professional studio" in Los Angeles. Ultimately, only "Foreplay/Long Time" and "Let Me Take You Home Tonight" contained future band members Barry Goudreau, Fran Sheehan (bass), and John "Sib" Hashian (drums). *Boston* went to #3 on the charts while launching three hit singles with "More Than a Feeling" (#5), "Foreplay/Long Time" (#22), and "Peace of Mind" (#38).

His perfectionism was both a boon and an impediment for Scholz and the band. He took two years to finish a follow-up, *Don't Look Back*, and only released it in 1978 after pressure from Epic. It promptly went to #1, though he was so dissatisfied with the results that he vowed to never be rushed again. During the interim, in 1980 the Scholz Research & Development company created first the Power Soak as a way to get the flat-out distorted sound of a cranked amp at low-volume levels as heard on the Boston albums, followed in 1982 by the immensely popular Rockman portable headphone guitar amp based on the Sony Walkman concept.

© Marty Temme

"They just knock the music because it's not their brand or they automatically don't like it because it was enormously successful."

—Tom Scholz responding to criticism of Boston

Aerosmith, the other Boston band, wanted to fly above the clouds, but the "Rockman" blasted his debut album into orbit with a mammoth sound and the attitude to go with it.

Subsequently, it took Scholz until 1986 for *Third Stage*, which topped out at #3, with only Delp remaining from the original band. Epic was not amused with the length of time between releases, and Scholz spent the next seven years defending himself against charges he had violated his contract. He prevailed and presented *Walk On* in 1994 as a virtual solo project and his first commercial failure. In 1995, Scholz sold his Rockman line of products to Dunlop.

In 2002, Scholz released the politically-themed *Corporate America*, with Delp guesting, which reached a respectable #42 on the charts; the preceding release of the title track became a hugely popular download online. Encouraged by the response to his latest opus, Scholz led the latest incarnation of his band on a two-year tour.

In 2007, Brad Delp, the voice of Boston, committed suicide, and the bereft Scholz presided over a tribute concert. He also guested with Stryper on their cover of "More Than a Feeling." In 2008, however, he requested that Republican presidential hopeful Mike Huckabee desist from using the song in his campaign.

How to Play It

Tom Scholz stretches his strings and his chops a little further in his second solo of 16 measures between interludes following verse 2. A two-measure chord sequence of F and Cm–E♭–B♭ appears in measures 1–14 with the F chord providing resolution in measures 15 and 16. The tonality is firmly grounded in F major, and Scholz relies heavily on the F minor pentatonic scale in several positions along with the F major pentatonic in the relative D minor pentatonic position as well as a few well-chosen notes from the F major scale, or Ionian mode. Powering it all is his patented Power Soak that allows him to crank the front end, or preamp section, of his Marshall for maximum blast and sustain while not exceeding acceptable volume levels in the studio.

After a sweeping bend from A♭ to B♭ on string 1 over the F chord in measure 1 to create musical tension, Scholz follows with a bend from B♭ to C in anticipation of and resolution to the Cm change in measure 2. From there on to the end of his solo, he employs an impressive variety of musical devices to produce a lasting monument of hard rock guitar. In measures 2–3, he trots out his flashiest repeating licks in the root-octave position of the F minor pentatonic scale to immediately pump up the energy. He then slips in a fluttering trill in measure 4 with the C and E♭ notes on string 2 from the previous measures and dive bombs precipitously before quickly launching a series of upper-register bends in measures 5–6 in thrilling contrast. Notice that the bend from C to D at fret 20 on string 1 manufactures palpable tension that is only increased in measures 7–8 where Scholz rockets down the root position of the D minor pentatonic scale. The result is a welcome change of sweet harmony and melody, though true resolution does not occur until measure 11. Meanwhile, Scholz dynamically descends to fret 5 on string 6 where he rumbles and growls among the A and B♭ notes in striking contrast to the soaring bends of measures 5 and 6. As if to further make his point, in measure 12 he picks the open 6th string and then dive bombs until the string literally goes slack.

In measure 13, Scholz comes up for air in the root position of the F major scale with an ascending F major arpeggio that leads to one of his trademark trills from C to the D on string 2 in measure 14. Next, he seamlessly modulates to the root position of the F minor pentatonic scale by moving up one fret on string 2 in measure 15 where he repeatedly bends the E♭ note up one step to the root F along with one snarky bend to the E natural as the major 7th on beat 2 for tension. In measure 16, instead of a neat and tidy resolution to F, Scholz opts instead to bend up the B♭ on string 3 at fret 3 to B♮ for tension and then to C with vibrato. The mild tension of the shimmering 5th makes the F5 and G5 power chords on beat 4 a dynamic, but not abrupt, succession of harmony ending the solo and leading into the interlude (not shown).

Vital Stats

Guitarist: Tom Scholz

Song: "Long Time"

Album: *Boston*

Age at time of recording: 29

Guitar: 1968 Les Paul Goldtop w/ DiMarzio Super Distortion humbucker in bridge position

Amp: Marshall 100 watt stack

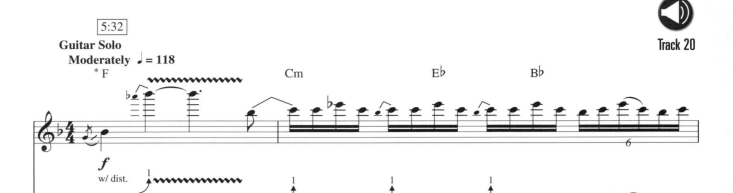

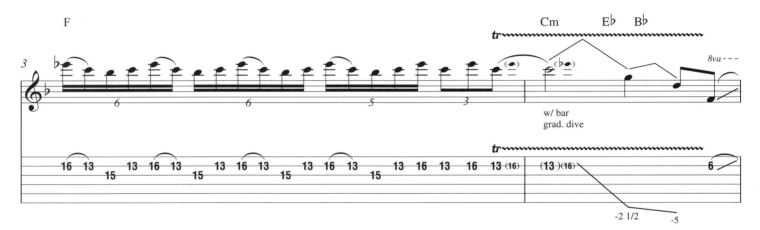

*Chord symbols reflect overall harmony.

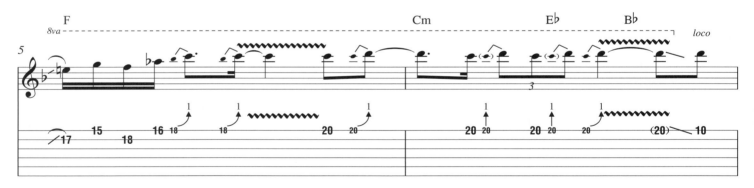

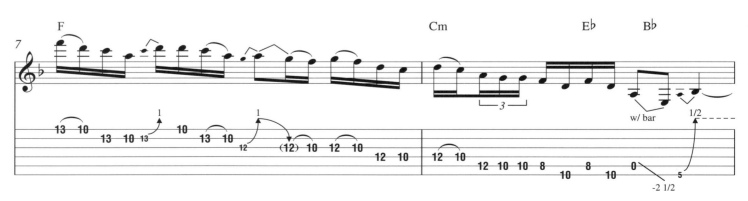

Words and Music by Tom Scholz
Copyright © 1976 Pure Songs
Copyright Renewed
All Rights Administered by Next Decade Entertainment, Inc.
All Rights Reserved   Used by Permission

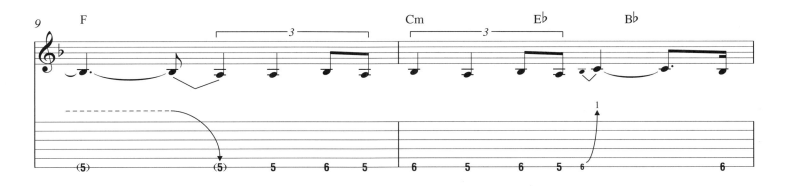

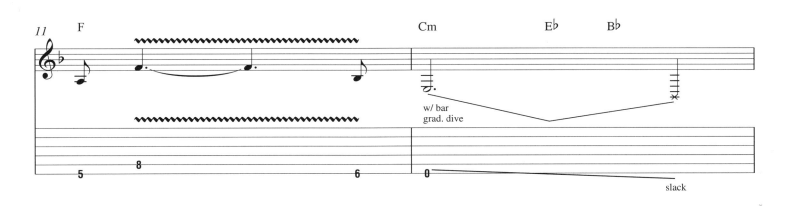

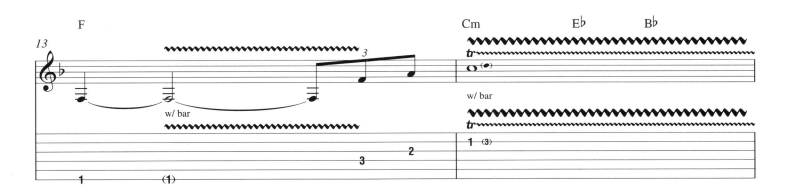

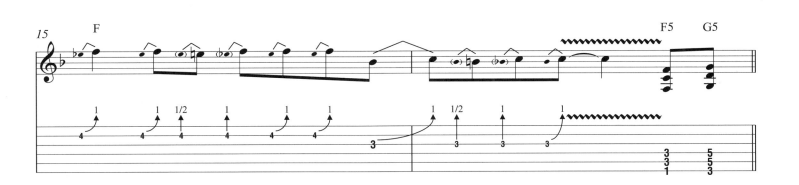

Bill Bartlett

© Getty

Ram Jam was not only a "one-hit wonder," but a studio band featuring the same lead guitarist, Bill Bartlett, and utilizing the same blistering up-tempo recording of "Black Betty" as tracked in 1976 by Starstruck from Cincinnati, Ohio. The first commercial recording of the song had been cut a capella in New York in 1939 by Huddie "Leadbelly" Ledbetter as a 0:55 long section of a medley of work songs with "Looky Looky Yonder" and "Yellow Woman's Doorbells." It was covered many times

"I told them it was about (fifties pin-up) Betty Paige."

—Bill Bartlett's response to the protests of the NAACP and CORE

after that, including by Leadbelly again in 1941 and Odetta in 1964.

William Ernest Bartlett was born in Dayton, Ohio on February 28, 1943, and became enamored with boogie woogie piano, especially the great Pete Johnson from Kansas City, when he was 11 and realized it would impress girls. He attended Syracuse University in upstate New York in the early sixties to study chemical engineering and play guitar before transferring to Miami University in Oxford, Ohio, where he became a member of the Lemon Pipers with his bluesy psychedelic guitar. In 1967, they were offered a contract from Buddah Records in New York and moved to the Big Apple. Bartlett became one of the main writers for the band, though not for their #1 "bubblegum" hit, "Green Tambourine," that the group was forced by management to record. They

dissolved in 1969 following further disagreements over material.

Bartlett moved back to Ohio and hooked up with Starstruck, a local Oxford band. In 1972, he heard the folk blues trio Kerner, Ray, and Glover do a version of "Black Betty," featuring all vocals and handclaps, and decided to create a heavy, blues-rocking version. Over time, along with the band, he fleshed out the arrangement, adding various guitar parts and going through many incarnations until it reached its final form. Released on the Truckstar label, it garnered local play and elicited wild reaction from fans. It was then heard by Epic Record producers Jerry Kasenetz and Jeff Katz in New York who had previously worked with the Ohio Express and the 1910 Fruitgum Company. Recognizing the potential of the tune and Bartlett, they recruited him, sans Starstruck, to sing lead, play guitar, and front a studio band christened Ram Jam. A dynamic and dramatic version of the song was brilliantly overdubbed and edited, and the second time proved to be the charm, as it went to #18 in 1977, creating a brief,

They neither rammed nor necessarily jammed, but were a studio band fronted by an exceptionally fiery and accomplished guitarist who touched a musical and cultural nerve with "Betty."

two-album recording and performing career for the band. However, Bartlett went back to Ohio to play in several Midwest bands and now lives in semi-retirement, playing piano in local bars and restaurants.

A controversy surrounded the release of "Black Betty" as both the NAACP and CORE protested the song as demeaning to black women and called for a boycott. In fact, the original lyrics likely are metaphorical as the term historically referred to, among other things, a flintlock musket with a black stock—hence the lyric, "bam-ba-lam." The rifle that followed it had a brown, unpainted stock and was the "baby" called "Brown Bess." "Black Betty" had also been the name for a bottle of whiskey, a whip, and the "Black Maria" that transferred penitentiary prisoners in the South.

Artists as diverse as Nick Cave, Tom Jones, and Spiderbait have subsequently recorded versions of Ram Jam's "Black Betty." Like "Rock and Roll" by Gary Glitter, it has been appropriated by sports teams as a rallying cry, including the New York Yankees, who played it during the 2008 All-Star Game.

How to Play It

Starting most prominently with "Light My Fire" in 1967, record companies began releasing edited "single" versions of album tracks deemed too long for radio play. Virtually without exception, it was the solos that got the axe, and such was the case with "Black Betty." Consequently, the album version is so radically different with the addition of the solo as to make it almost another song entirely.

Bill Bartlett takes it literally and figuratively to a new level during his 24-measure, high-speed, double-time romp that is subtly divided into two 12-measure sections. Understand that "double-time" indicates a tempo twice as fast as before. Charging ahead, Bartlett rips in a country-rock vein over D, D, G5, D5, B5, and B5 changes repeated twice, followed by D, D, B5, and B5 chords repeated six times. With consummate technical skill, especially considering the tempo, he brilliantly mixes the D major pentatonic and B minor pentatonic scales. As his basic soloing concept, Bartlett logically saves the root, extension, and higher positions of the B minor pentatonic scale for the B5 changes in measures 5, 6, 11, 12, 15, 16, 19, 20, 23, and 24. His goal in the solo, admirably achieved, is chest-thumping energy and overwhelming musical tension and anticipation along with the worthy musical concept of tension and release through note selection, as Bartlett does target the root notes at critical points along the way. An especially effective sequence occurs right off in measures 1–5 over the D, G5, D5, and B5 changes that lends an air of structure to go along with the blinding and accurate flatpicking. Observe that Bartlett sets the works in motion by pounding the F♯ (major 3rd) at fret 14 on string 1 in measures 1 and 2 to define the D major tonality while also engendering forward motion that the root D note would not accomplish.

To complement his fusillade of notes, Bartlett inserts dynamic measures containing punchy bends. Though not based on any apparent system or structure, his choice of when to employ them does have a certain rhythm that feels natural and organic. For instance, he inserts prominent bends in measures 6, 9, 11, 15–18, and 21–22. More significantly, Bartlett singles out the E note on string 2 at fret 17 for special attention. When he bends it one step in measures 11–12 over the B change, the resulting F♯ tone as the 5th functions to harmonize smoothly with the chord. In measures 15–16, where it is blended with the A note on string 1 at fret 17, a bluesy 7th harmony is produced. Similarly, in measures 17–18 over the D chord, the F♯ becomes the major 3rd, as in measures 1 and 2, harmonizing with and confirming the major tonality of the change. Be sure to observe, however, that in measures 21–22, the relatively languid bend of the E to the F♯ over the D5 chord in conjunction with the A note creates a D major double stop in 3rds for firm resolution. Combined with the slippery run down the root position of the B minor pentatonic scale in measures 23–24, it makes for a satisfying and logical climax to a breakneck, breathtaking solo.

Vital Stats

Guitarist: Bill Bartlett

Song: "Black Betty"

Album: *Ram Jam*

Age at time of recording: 31

Guitar: Customized Gibson Les Paul Standard

Amp: Marshall JTM45

Black Betty

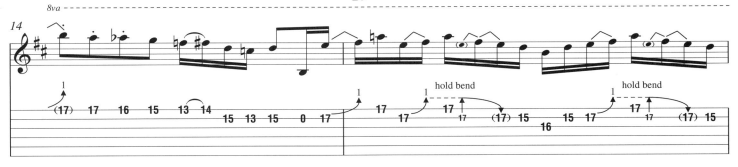

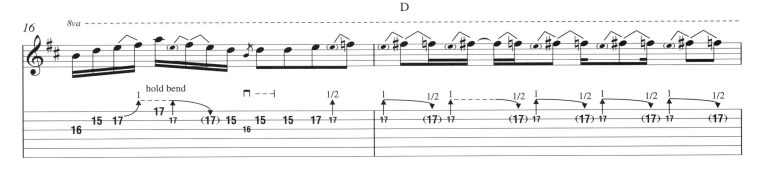

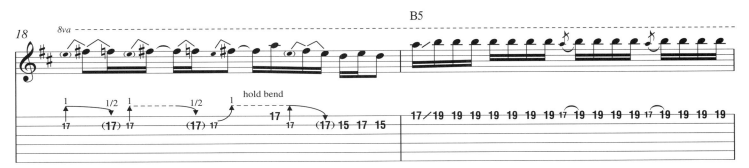

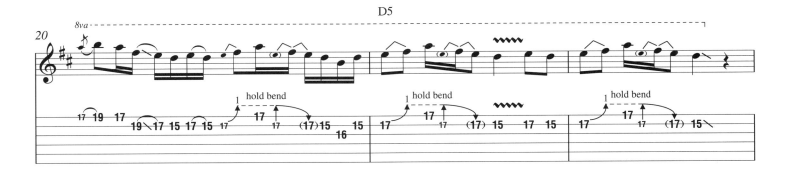

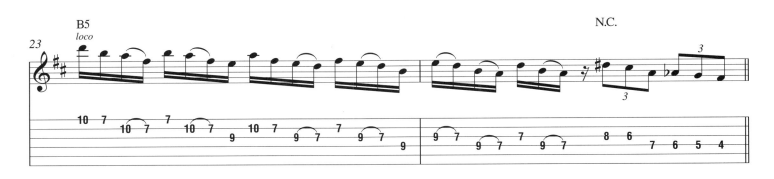

Michael Schenker

© Photofest

"My fun part is lead breaks, and I have a meaning behind each one of them and, therefore, I review my music differently than other people may do."

—Michael Schenker

The conventional wisdom in some circles is that the unprecedented creative flowering of improvisational rock that occurred in the sixties devolved into self-indulgence in the seventies—not to mention punk and disco music. Of the latter two there is no debate, of course, but a strong argument could be mounted against the first charge. One noteworthy development was the advanced chops of exceptionally fluid and melodic guitarists such as Michael Schenker of UFO.

Phil Mogg (vocals), Mick Bolton (guitar), Pete Way (bass), and Andy Parker (drums) formed the metal band Hocus Pocus in 1969 in England. In 1971, they changed their name to UFO and released *UFO 1* followed by *Flying* and *Live* (1972) that found substantial success in Japan and Europe, but very little in their native Great Britain. In 1974, Bolton left and Larry Wallis from Pink Fairies and future Whitesnake guitarist Bernie Marsden were given auditions. When Marsden forgot his passport on a UFO gig in Germany, Michael Schenker was enticed to join after being heard at a sound check for the Scorpions, the opening act led by his older brother Rudolph with whom he started as a 15-year-old *wunderkind* in 1970. He spoke virtually no English but single-handedly turned UFO's fortunes around on the hard rocking *Phenomenon* in 1974 with his writing and "phenomenal" playing.

Featuring his spectacular technique and modal melodicism throughout with the standouts "Doctor Doctor" and "Rock Bottom," as well as a credible cover of the Howlin' Wolf blues classic, "Built for Comfort," it also included him playing the melody with his feet on the instrumental "Lipstick Traces." *Force It* in 1975 and *No Heavy Petting* the following year raised the band's stock in the U.S. Keyboardist/guitarist Paul Raymond was inducted to fill out the sound for *Lights Out* in 1977 and *Obsession* in 1978, after which Schenker left following dissension with Mogg regarding his alcohol abuse and erratic behavior. In his wake, he also left the live *Strangers in the Night* from 1978 as a testament to his virtuosity before going off to rejoin the Scorpions in 1979 with Mathias Jabs filling in. The same year, he unsuccessfully "auditioned" with Aerosmith (!) when Joe Perry split and then went on to form various versions of the Michael Schenker Group in the eighties. In 1982, he again unsuccessfully "auditioned" to take the late Randy Rhoads' place with Ozzy Osbourne.

Michael Schenker shone a light on an evolving style featuring immaculate chops, a knowledge of the modes, and a dose of bluesy feel and phrasing.

Guitarist Phil Chapman, who had appeared on *Strangers in the Night*, took over for Schenker but could not fill the Aryan rock god's shoes. The band released *Mechanix* in 1982, after which bassist Pete Way left to form Waysted. *Making Contact* followed in 1983 to little support, and they broke up. In 1985, they reformed for *Misdemeanor*, only to pull the plug again shortly thereafter. In a scenario that would play itself out down to the present day, the original UFO lineup of Mogg, Way, Parker, Raymond, and Schenker got back together in 1995 for *Walk on the Water,* a tour, and then split up. Mogg and Way, as Mogg/Way, released *Edge of the World* in 1997 with guitarist George Bellas and veteran Brit drummer Aynsley Dunbar and *Chocolate Box* in 1999 with guitarist Jeff Kollman, marking time until Schenker returned in 2000 for *Covenant* and *Sharks* in 2002. Naturally, Schenker ran off to release solo albums in the nineties, and Dunbar high-tailed it as well. They were replaced by Vinnie Moore and Jason Bonham, respectively, along with returning keyboard man Raymond for *You Are Here* in 2004 and the live *Showtime* in 2005. In 2006, Bonham left, and the original drummer Parker rejoined again for *The Monkey Puzzle*.

How to Play It

As was and is his M.O., Michael Schenker combines speed, impeccable execution, and a finely-tuned ear for melody over the simplest modal chord changes to produce memorable solos of great expression and emotional depth. A prime factor of his art is rubbery vibrato that he applies liberally, particularly to his bends to the root as seen in measures 1–6 with the E to F♯ note on string 2 at fret 17 over the F♯5.

Check out how quickly Schenker goes from 0 to 100 MPH after entering "economically" with the bends in measure 1. Continuing to utilize the F♯ minor pentatonic scale in the root-octave position at fret 14, he spews sixteenth notes as fast and clean as other virtuosos play more common eighth notes. As is the concept in modal soloing where one scale is used over one chord or tonal center, he creates searing tension in measures 1–8 with speed demon licks revolving around the F♯ note. Pay attention to the way his restricted note selection of the top three strings of the scale further concentrates the focus and musical tension in the upper register. In measures 7 and 8, he floors it for the climax of the F♯ section with exceedingly zippy pull-offs to fret 14 on strings 1 and 2 that serve to highlight the root F♯ and C♯ (5th) notes, respectively. In addition, see how Schenker makes a definite end in measure 8 with the sustained F♯ note as resolution and a gliss upwards from the E note on string 2 at fret 5.

Measures 9–16 contain a chord change from the F♯5 to C♯5, the V chord, to contribute to the driving momentum of the rhythm. A feeling of "uplift" is intensified as Schenker relocates to the root position of the C♯ Dorian mode at fret 9 to firmly acknowledge the change of tonality. Be aware that, though the Dorian mode is a minor scale, the C♯5 "power chord," being theoretically neither major nor minor, allows for a wide selection of scale choices—a fact not lost on heavy rock and metal guitarists! As in measures 1–8, Schenker quickly establishes his new chord change, or key change as in this example, with the root C♯ note in measure 9 by bending up to it from B on string 2 at fret 12. Do not miss that the B was accessed by the gliss on beat 4 of measure 8.

As opposed to measures 1–8, where he pretty much kept the "pedal to the metal" with supercharged sixteenth notes from start to finish, Schenker structures the second part of his solo with a beginning, middle, and end. Measures 9–10 find him "easing" in with the repetition of the bends to C♯, while in measures 11–13 he quickly turns up the wick and emphasizes the half-step notes in the C♯ Dorian mode on strings 1 and 2 to create fluid, melodic runs and riffs. In measure 14, however, he dynamically descends the scale with a whoosh and then reverses direction in measure 15 as he hurtles towards the climax of his solo in measure 16 with the repeating double stops of C♯/G♯ on strings 1 and 2 at fret 9. Completing the cycle begun in measure 9, Schenker ends on the B bent up to C♯ on string 2 at fret 12.

Vital Stats

Guitarist: Michael Schenker

Song: "Lights Out"

Album: *Lights Out* – UFO

Age at time of recording: 22

Guitar: 1975 Gibson Flying V

Amp: Marshall 50 watt stack

2:00

Guitar Solo
Moderately fast Rock ♩ = 152

F#5

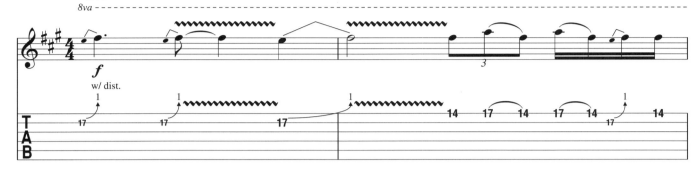

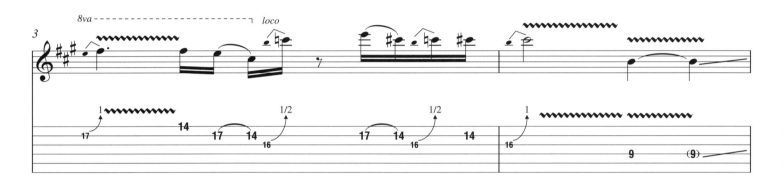

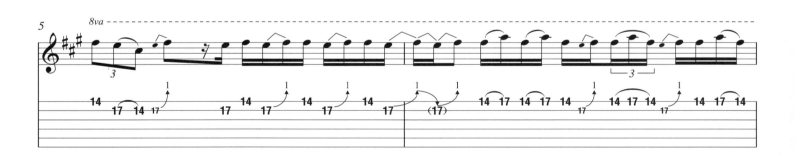

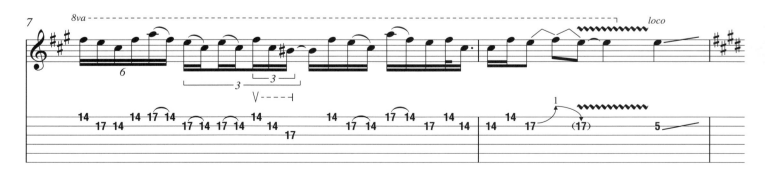

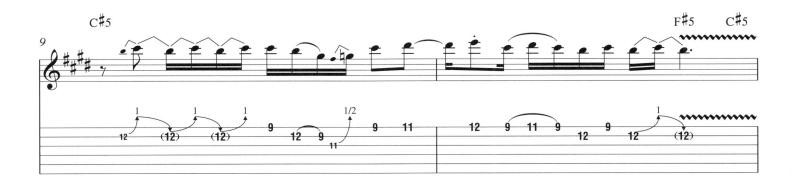

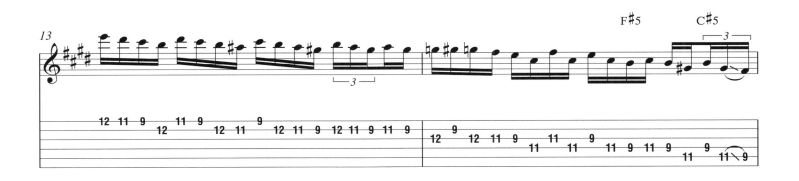

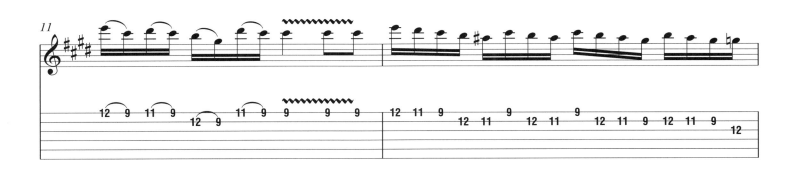

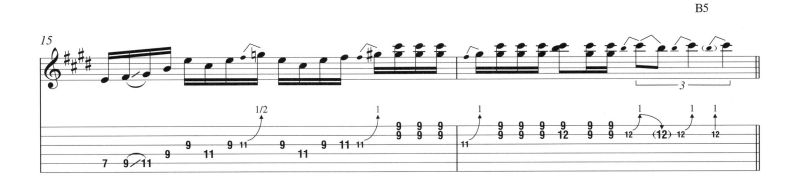

Brian May

© Marty Temme

Queen, from England, blurred the distinction between more musical categories than any other band in the seventies. With a flaming glam rock front-man writing wildly progressive and eclectic rock material and a virtuoso guitarist with melodic heavy metal leanings and genius for layered guitar parts, they reigned with an iron hand in a velvet glove.

Queen formed in 1970 in London when guitarist Brian May and drummer Roger Taylor from the psychedelic band Smile recruited Farrokh Bulsara, aka "Freddie Mercury," from Wreckage to replace their departing singer. With bassist John Deacon in 1971, they rehearsed for two years while all four completed college educations. Mercury came up with the name Queen, coyly acknowledging that it "…was open to all sorts of interpretations." In 1973, they released their self-titled debut album (#83) to critical praise but scant sales, even in Great Britain where a loyal fanbase would eventually develop and make them bigger than the Beatles. *Queen II* (#49) in 1974 reached #5 in their homeland but received more of the same indifference in the U.S. *Sheer Heart Attack* (#12) at the end of 1974, though, went gold with "Killer Queen" (#12) featuring bombastic hard rock coupled with Mercury's campy lyrics and theatrical performances.

The "stage" was literally set for their greatest triumphs beginning in 1976. The triple-platinum *A Night at the Opera* (#4), with the humorously operatic "Bohemian Rhapsody" (#11) and "You're My Best friend" (#16), was expensive, outrageous, overblown, and an instant classic. *A Day at the Races* (#5), also named for a Marx Brothers movie, a year later with "Somebody to Love" (#13) and "Tie Your Mother Down" (#49), was a less ambitious version of its predecessor. The far-reaching *News of the World* (#3) in 1978 has had "We Will Rock You" (#4 and #52 in 1992) and "We Are the Champions" (#4) appropriated and immortalized by sports teams around the world as their anthems.

With *Jazz* (#6) in 1979 featuring "Fat Bottomed Girls/Bicycle Race" (#24) and "Don't Stop Me Now" (#86), Queen

The "news" for guitar players was that Brian May seemed to have an endless string of innovative harmonic and melodic ideas to spring on the rock world.

"I had this thing about guitar harmonies. I wanted to be the first to put proper three-part harmonies onto a record. That was an achievement."

—Brian May

continued the diverse mix of styles, reflecting the individual band members' tastes. *The Game* (#1) in 1980 proved their bank-ability in the U.S. and was more pop than rock with a broad range of material as exemplified by the neo-rockabilly "Crazy Little Thing Called Love" (#1) and the disco hit "Another One Bites the Dust" (#1, and #2 on Black Singles chart). Unfortunately, it also marked the start of a gradual downhill slide. "Under Pressure" (#29) in 1981 produced by David Bowie helped, but the synth-driven dance rock of *Hot Space* (#22) in 1982 and *The Works* (#23) in 1984 were seen as pandering to the "new wave."

A spectacular performance at Live Aid in 1985 was a boost, but *A Kind of Magic* (#46) the next year was not, and *The Miracle* (#24) in 1989 was not quite, either. The gold *Innuendo* (#30) from 1991 succeeded like their seventies classics, but their lack of gigs was an ominous sign. On November 23, Mercury announced he had AIDs and died the next day. May and Taylor went on to pursue solo projects, as Deacon virtually retired. In 2001, they were inducted into the Rock and Roll Hall of Fame. In 2005, Paul Rodgers, formerly of Free and Bad Company, joined Queen for *Return of the Champions* (#84) and *The Cosmos Rocks* (#47) in 2008 to indifferent response.

How to Play It

Among electric guitarists, it is considered the highest achievement to develop a personal style and tone that is instantly recognizable. Brian May is an honored member of that select and exclusive club that includes B.B. King, Albert King, Jimi Hendrix, Jeff Beck, Eric Clapton, and Duane Allman, among other worthy luminaries. Adding to the distinction, he built his signature solid-body guitar named "Red Special" with his father around the age of seven.

May pummels a 9-measure outro guitar solo following Queen's raucous and pugnacious classic sing-a-long "We Will Rock You" over just hand claps and feet stomping that has become a tradition at sporting events in a manner similar to Gary Glitter's "Rock and Roll Pt. 2." Essentially a I–IV vamp of A–D changes, the solo is an excellent tutorial in how to build a powerhouse musical statement around the typical rock guitar A major barre-chord voicing at fret 2 accessed with the index finger and the octave voicing at fret 14.

After fading in on the sustained E note on string 3 at fret 9 with swelling feedback and explosive open A chords at the end of the vocal section (not shown), May relies in measure 1 on the trusty country blues riff of pulling down one quarter step with the middle finger on the G note on string 6 to the "true blue" note between G and G♯ preceding the A chord. In the blink of an eye, he then whips up to the octave A/E second inversion in measure 2 where he waxes rhythmically creative to the end of the solo, often including the open 5th string as a pedal tone. His favorite maneuver that is repeated as a motif occurs in measures 2, 3, 4, 6, 7, 8, and 9 as a hammer-on from A to D/F♯ to imply a quick D change. Observe how his distorted tone is reminiscent of bagpipes. Jimi Hendrix was wont to occasionally use this form in songs like "Wait Until Tomorrow," but

the guitarist most closely identified with its use is Keith Richards. Starting around *Let It Bleed* in 1969, it would provide the foundation for "Gimme Shelter," "Brown Sugar," Tumbling Dice," and "Start Me Up," among other Stones classics.

Balancing the ultra-aggressive chord forms are single-note lines in measures 3, 4, and 5 derived from the A Mixolydian mode that conveniently connect to the octave form of the A/E voicing at fret 14. The dynamic effect of contrasting short melodies with the incessant harmony is one of the main factors that contribute to the esteemed status of the solo. Check out the squawking bends and pull-offs in measure 5 that lend a bluesy touch and contribute welcome, if brief, rhythmic contrast to the mainly straight sixteenth- and eighth-note licks. By measure 9, however, May is beating on the A and D voicings with undisguised glee as he brings his instrumental break to a "rocking" conclusion.

Vital Stats

Guitarist: Brian May

Song: "We Will Rock You"

Album: *News of the World* – Queen

Age at time of recording: 30

Guitar: "Red Special," home-made custom solidbody electric

Amp: Vox AC30TBX

Words and Music by Brian May

Eddie Van Halen

In the late seventies, Eddie Van Halen arrived on the scene with a wildly original hard rock style based on volume, athletic licks, and eclectic melodies. The fans agreed, and through 2007, his band has sold more than 80 million records worldwide.

By the early seventies, Edward Lodewijk Van Halen and his brother Alex were playing guitar and drums in Mammoth around Pasadena, California. Singer David Lee Roth joined as did bassist Michael Anthony, and by 1974, they were dubbed "Van Halen," gigging incessantly around Los Angeles. In 1977, after two failed demos, they were signed to Warner Bros. Records.

The platinum *Van Halen* (#19) in 1978, with "Runnin' with the Devil" (#84) and the Kinks cover "You Really Got Me" (#36), segued from the epochal "Eruption," spawned legions of imitators. *Van Halen II* (#6) the

One look at Eddie Van Halen's hot-modded Strat on the debut album cover was a warning for guitarists to be prepared for something radically different, and VH did not disappoint.

following year sported "Dance the Night Away" (#15) and "Beautiful Girls" (#84). The all-original *Women and Children First* (#6) in 1980 contained "And the Cradle Will Rock" (#55). *Fair Warning* (#5 in 1981) reflected their growing popularity and the growing tensions between Roth and Eddie. *Diver Down* (#3) a year later, with "Dancing in the Street" (#38) and "Oh, Pretty Woman" (#12), was a mash up of covers and originals.

The massively successful *1984* (#2) from the same year boasted their first #1 single in "Jump" along with "Panama" (#13), "I'll Wait" (#13), and "Hot for Teacher" (#56) and is considered their commercial high point. However, when Roth delayed the follow-up to do his own successful solo album in 1985, he was fired. Fans protested, but Sammy Hagar was brought in for *5150* in 1986, which, surprisingly, shot to #1, featuring "Why Can't This Be Love?" (#3), "Love Walks In" (#22), "Dreams" (#22), and "Best of Both Worlds"; surprisingly, the Hagar era produced the biggest Van Halen hits. *OU812* in 1988 repeated at #1 with "Black and Blue" (#37), "Finish What Ya Started" (#13), "When It's Love" (#5), and "Feels So Good" (#35). The Grammy-winning *For Unlawful Carnal Knowledge* ("F.U.C.K.") became the band's third straight #1 with Hagar, containing "Top of the World" (#27) and "Right Now" (#55) in 1991.

© Marty Temme

Following the double-disc *Van Halen Live: Right Here, Right Now* (#5) in 1993, the band released *Balance* (#1) in 1995 with "Can't Stop Loving You" (#30) and "Not Enough" (#97) for their fourth studio chart-topper. Eddie's recent sobriety clashed with Hagar's boozing, however, and after Roth was brought in surreptitiously to record, Hagar left in 1996. A reunion with Roth fell through, and former Extreme singer Gary

"I didn't even play it right. There's a mistake at the top of it."

—Eddie talking about "Eruption"

Cherone was hired for *Van Halen III* (#4) in 1998. It was their poorest-selling album to date, Cherone left amicably, and Eddie had hip replacement surgery in 1999. Rumors in 2001 about another Roth/Van Halen reunion surfaced when he described new recorded tracks, but news of Eddie's battle with oral cancer quashed them, and it was stated that they had not decided on their next singer.

The next few years were unsettled, as both Roth and Hagar joined the Heavyweight Champs of Rock 'n' Roll tour. In 2004, Hagar returned to Van Halen for an American tour, but he and Anthony went back to the Warboritas in 2005. In 2007, the band was inducted into the Rock and Roll Hall of Fame, once again fueling rumors of a reunion with Roth that proved true when a financially-successful tour, interrupted by Eddie's lack of sobriety, was launched in the fall with his son Wolfgang on bass.

How to Play It

Eddie Van Halen has been a major electric guitar innovator with talent flowing from his imaginative intuition and an uninhibited and flashy concept of soloing. In his version of the Kinks' British Invasion blues rock classic, he gives short shrift to the original solo (still debated as to whether it was played by Kink axe-man Dave Davies or former session guitarist Jimmy Page) while injecting a selection of his classic moves.

The solo is 12 measures long but is not constructed from standard I, IV, and V blues changes, or the form of the verse (not shown). Instead, it consists of three four-measure phrases, each of which do contain the signature one-measure vamp of A–G–A for the first three measures, while ending on the fourth with a different harmony. Van Halen comes roaring in with a vengeance in measures 1–4, beginning with the explosive classic rock lick of the A/E double stop in the root position of the minor pentatonic scale, beloved by blues artists as well as Chuck Berry, in order to claim the A tonality. As a transition, he plays the typical blues bend of the 4th (D) to the 5th (E) in measure 2, as in the original before launching into measure 3 where he displays his phenomenal tapping technique to breathtaking effect. Dig how he expands his scale palette to include notes associated with the Dorian and Aeolian modes for long, descending melodic lines that go by at a blinding pace. Also notice how he chooses to exit the tapping with a visit to the A major pentatonic scale voiced in the root position of the F♯ minor pentatonic scale as a set up for the dynamic shift in register that follows.

Van Halen zooms to the root-octave position of the A minor pentatonic scale in measures 5–8 where his stratospheric bends produce the greatest musical tension in contrast to the tightly compressed licks that preceded. A spectacular two-step bend in measure 5 of G to B at fret 20 on string 2 is a stunning leap in register and an early climactic moment in the solo. Maintaining

his focus with Herculean bends as opposed to speed, Van Halen begins wrenching the E note on string 2 at fret 17 in measure 7 after relocating to the root-octave position of the F♯ minor pentatonic scale. The one-and-a-half step bends to G are superseded by a gigantic Albert King-type "choke" of two-and-a-half steps to A on beat 3 of measure 7, followed by a whopping two-step bend of C to E on string 3 at fret 17 in measure 8.

A multi-step bend of E to F♯ and then G in measure 9 functions as a final burst of musical tension as Van Halen sustains the note to the edge of feedback over measures 10–12 while simultaneously flicking his toggle switch on and off for a stuttering, Hendrix-like effect. The result is a dynamic and breathless winding down of the hyperkinetic energy of the solo on the way towards the interlude (not shown), where the band, save for drummer Alex Van Halen, drops out as singer David Lee Roth ad libs.

Vital Stats

Guitarist: Eddie Van Halen

Song: "You Really Got Me"

Album: *Van Halen*

Age at time of recording: 23

Guitar: Modified Ibanez Destroyer

Amp: 1967–68 100 watt Marshall

1:23

Tune down 1/2 step:
(low to high) E♭-A♭-D♭-G♭-B♭-E♭

Guitar Solo
Moderate Rock ♩ = 140

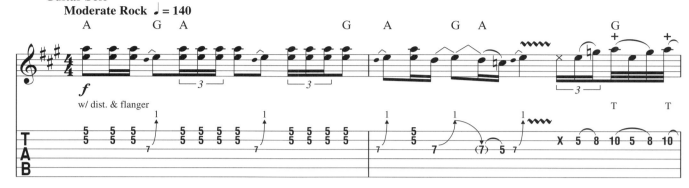

w/ dist. & flanger

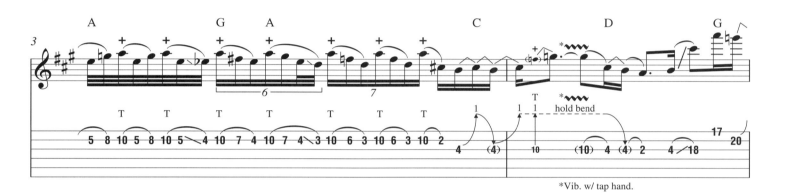

*Vib. w/ tap hand.

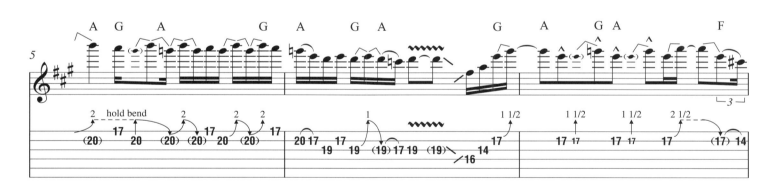

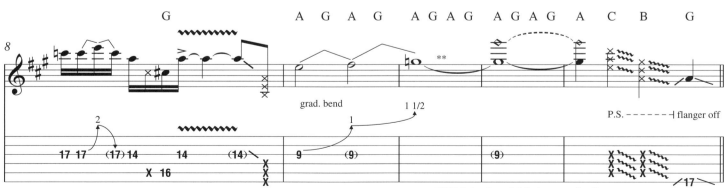

**Flick toggle switch between on & off
pickup selection to create stutter effect.

Pat Travers & Pat Thrall

© Marty Temme

Lauded and revered blues guru Pat Travers "lives the life he loves and loves the life he lives." As a dedicated hard rock and heavy blues guitarist, he continues to play his uncompromising version of the music with undiminished passion and is an acknowledged influence on both Paul Gilbert and Kirk Hammett.

Patrick Henry Travers was born on April 12, 1954, in Toronto, Canada. He started playing the guitar around the age of 12 after the life-changing experience of seeing Jimi Hendrix perform in Ottawa, Canada. With additional inspiration from British rock stars Eric Clapton, Jimmy Page, and Jeff Beck, who had all "gained their wings" in the Yardbirds, Travers set out to soar in his teens with a number of local bands around Quebec. When his band Merge was heard by Ronnie Hawkins, the Canadian blues and rockabilly legend took the young buck out on the road in the early seventies as his lead guitarist. After a year of paying dues in the blues, country, and fifties rock 'n' roll, Travers felt constrained and opted to go to hip London in 1975, where he hooked up with Peter "Mars" Cowling (bass) and Roy Dyke (drums) to bust a move up and down the length of Great Britain.

"From the streets of Toronto to the streets of London. Here to kick your ass, the Pat Travers Band."

—*Live! The Pat Travers Band*

In 1976, he cut a demo that became his first release for Polydor Records, *Pat Travers*, with a selection of choice covers, including Little Walter's "(Boom Boom) Out Go the Lights," which became his signature tune. The following year, with future Iron Maiden drummer Nicko McBrain, he released *Makin' Magic* and *Putting It Straight*. The former looked sharp at #70 and encouraged a move back to North America to go after the prized U.S. rock fan. With Cowling in tow, he recruited fiery second guitarist Pat Thrall from Automatic Man and former Black Oak Arkansas drummer Tommy Aldridge for *Heat in the Street* (1978), which broke in at #99. During a U.S. tour in 1979, he recorded the songs for his sensational *Live! Go for What You Know* (#29), roundly considered his peak performance, along with the even higher charting *Crash and Burn* (#20) in 1980. Unfortunately, the skinny tie new wavers in the eighties relegated Travers and his ilk to near extinction. He could not even ride the coattails of Stevie Ray Vaughan and Robert Cray during the second blues revival, however, and his last charting albums in the U.S. included *Radio Active*

The title was more than a little prescient as changing public tastes would shoot the explosive heavy blues rock of Travers and Thrall down to an early flame out.

(#37 in 1981), *Black Pearl* (#74 in 1982), and *Hot Shot* (#108 in 1984) with changes of personnel.

Even though his albums got progressively slicker, Travers' run near the top was over. On top of that, he had an ongoing beef with Polydor Records and ended up taking a hiatus from recording until 1990. *School of Hard Knocks* and succeeding releases failed to recapture his larger audience, but he kept slugging it out for his loyal fans (known as "Hammer Heads"). A series of blues albums for Blues Bureau, featuring the standouts *Blues Tracks* (1992) and *Blues Magnet* (1994), brought him back to his roots as did a few live discs showing his prowess during the nineties. Travers shows no signs of slowing down in the new millennium, performing with the Voices of Classic Rock and releasing a steady stream of albums, including *P.T. Power Trip* (2003) with bassist Gunter Nezhoda and veteran British blues drummer Aynsley Dunbar. In addition, he produced three albums with veteran rock drummer Carmen Appice in 2004 and 2005. He currently lives in Florida with his wife Monica, who sings backup with him, and their two children.

Ace co-guitarist Patrick Allen Thrall was born on August 26, 1953, in Alameda County, California, and raised in San Francisco. In 1976, he played in Stomo Yamashta's band Go, which also featured Steve Winwood and former Santana drummer Michael Shrieve. Adventurous and progressive from the start, he formed Automatic Man while still with Go, releasing two acclaimed albums. After establishing his name as a versatile guitarist and playing fusion music with

artists Narada Michael Walden and Alphonso Johnson, he joined Pat Travers in 1978 after passing an audition featuring 70 other guitarists. Following three albums and being named Best New Talent in *Guitar Player* magazine in 1980, he left Travers in 1981 to play with former Deep Purple vocalist/bassist Glenn Hughes in Hughes/Thrall. Despite great expectations, following a debut album and unreleased demos for a second release, they split up in 1982.

Since then, Thrall has played with Asia and Meatloaf while making a real name for himself as a producer. He has become an acknowledged expert at using Pro Tools and other digital technology, working with artists as diverse as Elton John, Bono, Joe Satriani, Tina Turner, and Queen. For a time in the nineties, his base of operations was at Studio PT at the Hit Factory in New York City. In 2005, he played on *Guitar Farm*, a tribute album of Northern California guitarists from Steve Woolverton, and in 2006, appeared with Joe Bonamassa on his *You & Me* album. In 2007, the remastered *I Got Your Number* from Hughes/Thrall in 1982 was released, including two recently re-recorded bonus tracks. Thrall currently lives in Las Vegas, Nevada, where he has a studio at the Palms.

How to Play It

The title purportedly came from a band member who showed up late for a rehearsal and offered as an excuse that he was "snortin' whiskey and drinkin' cocaine." The pure rock 'n' roll sass of the answer is the perfect introduction to second guitarist Pat Thrall's wildly uninhibited playing. His solo is 10 measures long and follows a typical 12-bar blues progression to measure 9, after which he inserts the VI (F#5) chord in measure 10 that leads into the interlude (not shown). The majority of the solo is spent in the root-octave position of the A blues scale at fret 17 with a nasty overdriven tone and exceptionally aggressive riffing that borders on musical violence.

A hallmark of Thrall (and Travers' style, for that matter) is the screaming bend and he makes a grand entrance in measure 1 with a whopping two-step example on beats 1–2 consisting of the ♭7th G note raised up to the hip 9th B that is actually begun in measure 12 of the preceding bridge (not shown). From there on to the climax of the solo, Thrall plays something dynamically different in virtually every measure as his goal is an all-out attack on the senses. In measure 2, he flips on down the scale, while in measure 3, he bends the G note at fret 20 one step to the root A for resolution and one-and-a-half steps to A♯ for ear-tweaking tension. In stunning contrast, measure 4 contains a unison bend on the E note at fret 17 and the F note at fret 18 delivered at warp speed as he builds tremendous momentum to the D major tonality-defining F♯ at fret 19 in measure 5 over the D chord. Do not miss how Thrall briefly accesses the D major pentatonic scale in the octave B minor pentatonic position on beats 3 and 4 of measure 5. In measure 6 over the D chord, he pulls a surprising move out of his bursting bag of tricks when he runs up the hip E♭ diminished scale on beat 1 before smoothly blending back into the root-octave position of the A blues scale at fret 17. Dig that the diminished scale (harmonized in unnerving tritones by Gtr. 2) is played one half step above the key (D) and contains altered blues notes relative to the key.

Measures 7–8 find Thrall utilizing his best Albert King lick when he executes a screaming howl with the double-string

bend of C/G up one step to D/A for overwhelming tension. Then, once again he shifts his tactics with a spectacular contrasting lick, slowly releasing a bend on string 3 from D to E at fret 7 in the root position of the A minor pentatonic scale while tapping with his right-hand index finger on the octave D note. Not content yet with his technical accomplishment as a fitting climax, Thrall swoops back up to the root-octave position of the A minor pentatonic scale for a squealing, sound barrier-breaking bend of one-and-a-half steps, followed by a buzzing pick scrape down the low E string.

Following the funky interlude (not shown), Pat Travers incorporates a Leslie-like effect and takes his turn while picking up the pace with a jam-packed four measures of adrenalin-laced riffing over the funky A7♯9 chord. Relying on his stone blues phrasing gathered and honed over many years of working "in the trenches," he tortures his strings for two measures in the root-octave position of the A minor pentatonic scale and two measures in the root position at fret 5. Measure 1 contains a classic blues harmony bend with the D at fret 19 on string 3 bent one step to E, while the pinky finger holds down the F at fret 20 on string 2 for a thrilling "train whistle" imitation. The musical tension created is dynamically countered in measure 2 with impossibly fast hammer-on licks involving the G, A, and C notes for yet even more tension, courtesy of the latter ♭3rd blues note.

Travers repeats the "train whistle" harmony bend one octave lower in measure 3. Not only does it function as a repeating motif that contributes structure to his short solo, but it contrasts with the

hammer-ons in measure 2 and keeps the fires stoked. Finally, Travers relents briefly on beats 2 and 3 with quick resolution to the A note on string 4 at fret 7. However, he concludes the measure on beat 4 with the aforementioned C note that is intensified with vibrato for more poignant musical tension and anticipation. Devilishly, Travers does not deliver resolution in measure 4; instead he ups the ante, trumping his buddy Thrall with a virtuosic "sleight-of-hand" display as the band drops out for maximum drama. Bending the D to E at fret 7 on string 3, he taps fret 10 with his right-hand ring finger while maintaining the bend. He then slides up string 3 with the same tapping finger and executes a slick pull-off back to D where his waiting fret-hand ring finger pulls off to C—all done in the blink of an eye. The slithery maneuver leads smoothly to an equally rapid pull-off from A to G on string 4 at fret 7, preceding a merciful return to the verse that follows.

Vital Stats

Guitarist: Pat Travers and Pat Thrall

Song: "Snortin' Whiskey"

Album: *Crash and Burn* – Pat Travers Band

Age at time of recording: Travers 26; Thrall 27

Guitar: 1957 Gibson Melody Maker w/ humbucking pickups; (Travers)
Paul Reed Smith (Thrall)

Amp: Travers and Thrall – 50 watt Marshall

* Catch 3rd string under bend finger.

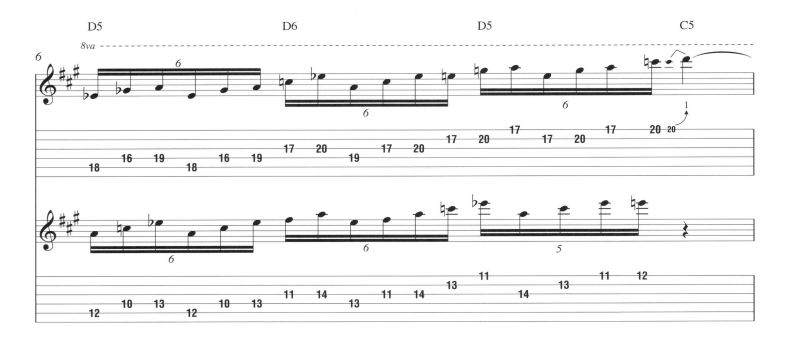

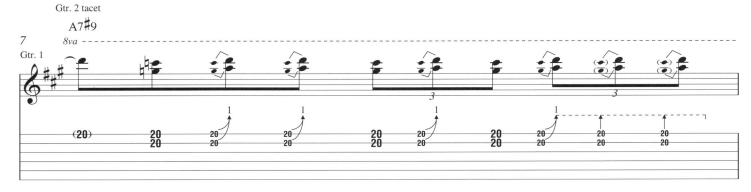

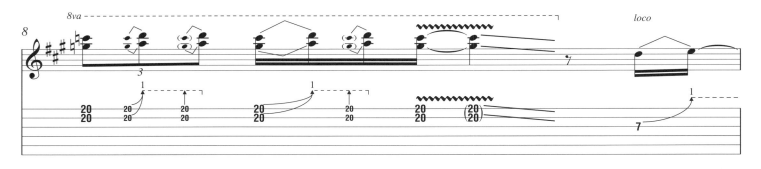

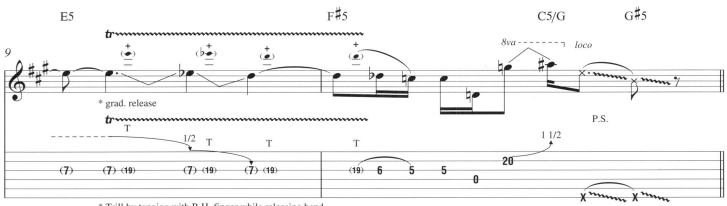

* Trill by tapping with R.H. finger while releasing bend.

2:27

Guitar Solo
Moderately ♩ = 104

A7#9

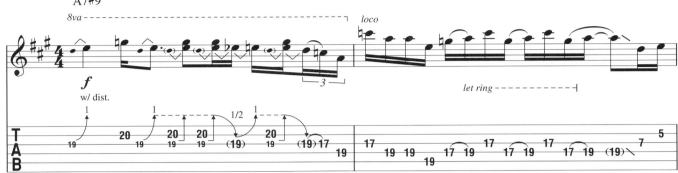

* Slide & pull off w/ tapping finger.

Conclusion

As one works their way through the book chronologically as presented, a relatively comprehensive course of study will materialize. Even taking into account the brilliantly subtle syncopation in the phrasing of Mike Mitchell in "Louie, Louie," it makes for an excellent starting point and introduction to the glories of rambunctious early sixties rock. The jump to "Jeff's Boogie" in the mid-sixties adds a swing element to the basic bluesy rock of its predecessor. In addition, it ups the chops ante due to Beck's speedy runs, while helping to prepare for the Latin jazz of Carlos Santana in "Soul Sacrifice" and all that follows in the late sixties and early seventies. Likewise, the psychedelic rock of Cream's "White Room," with Eric Clapton wah-wahing like crazy, leads logically to the soaring blues rock of "Train Kept A-Rollin'," courtesy of studio ace Steve Hunter. By the time a guitarist has absorbed all the previous lessons, the explosive and heavy hard rock of the two Pats—Travers and Thrall—in "Snortin' Whiskey" in 1980, feels like graduate school, with the "student" fully educated to go out and rock the world.

Part of the beauty of rock guitar is the way it encompasses the full width and breadth of popular music. Though the blues is clearly the single most important influence, country, folk, Tin Pan Alley, Latin, jazz, and even a smattering of classical music (as in the music of Queen), winds it way throughout the rich history of the genre. Going hand in hand with the multiculturalism is the egalitarianism that allows virtually anyone to pick up a guitar and wail away, no matter their background, experience, or level of expertise. All that is needed is the burning desire to burn!

About the Author

Dave Rubin is a New York City blues guitarist, teacher, author, and journalist. He has played with Son Seals, Honeyboy Edwards, Chuck Berry, Steady Rollin' Bob Margolin, Billy Boy Arnold, Johnny Copeland, James Brown's JBs, and the Campbell Brothers, among others. In addition, he has performed on the *Blues Alley* TV show in Philadelphia and *New York Now* in New York City and has appeared in commercials for Mountain Dew and the Oreck company.

Dave has been an author for the Hal Leonard Corporation for 20 years and currently has nine titles in his *Inside the Blues* series to go along with his numerous *Signature Licks* and *Guitar School* series and other assorted titles. He was the musical director for Star Licks DVD series *Legends of the Blues* and a Johnny Winter instructional DVD for Cherry Lane Music. His *12-Bar Blues* book/DVD package (Hal Leonard) was nominated for a Paul Revere Award in 1999.

As a journalist he currently writes for *Guitar Edge* and has written for *Guitar One*, *Living Blues*, *Blues Access*, *Guitar School*, *Guitar Shop*, *Guitar*, *Guitar Player*, and *Guitar World* magazines. Dave was the recipient of the 2005 Keeping the Blues Alive award in journalism from the Blues Foundation in Memphis, Tennessee.

Guitar Notation Legend

Guitar music can be notated three different ways: on a *musical staff*, in *tablature*, and in *rhythm slashes*.

RHYTHM SLASHES are written above the staff. Strum chords in the rhythm indicated. Use the chord diagrams found at the top of the first page of the transcription for the appropriate chord voicings. Round noteheads indicate single notes.

THE MUSICAL STAFF shows pitches and rhythms and is divided by bar lines into measures. Pitches are named after the first seven letters of the alphabet.

TABLATURE graphically represents the guitar fingerboard. Each horizontal line represents a string, and each number represents a fret.

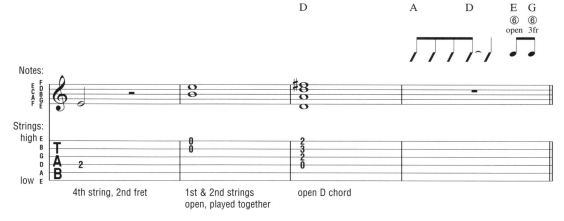

4th string, 2nd fret • 1st & 2nd strings open, played together • open D chord

Definitions for Special Guitar Notation

HALF-STEP BEND: Strike the note and bend up 1/2 step.

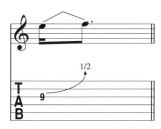

WHOLE-STEP BEND: Strike the note and bend up one step.

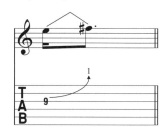

GRACE NOTE BEND: Strike the note and immediately bend up as indicated.

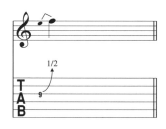

SLIGHT (MICROTONE) BEND: Strike the note and bend up 1/4 step.

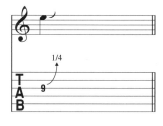

BEND AND RELEASE: Strike the note and bend up as indicated, then release back to the original note. Only the first note is struck.

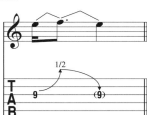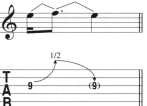

PRE-BEND: Bend the note as indicated, then strike it.

PRE-BEND AND RELEASE: Bend the note as indicated. Strike it and release the bend back to the original note.

UNISON BEND: Strike the two notes simultaneously and bend the lower note up to the pitch of the higher.

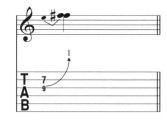

VIBRATO: The string is vibrated by rapidly bending and releasing the note with the fretting hand.

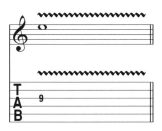

WIDE VIBRATO: The pitch is varied to a greater degree by vibrating with the fretting hand.

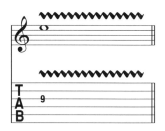

HAMMER-ON: Strike the first (lower) note with one finger, then sound the higher note (on the same string) with another finger by fretting it without picking.

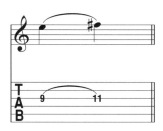

PULL-OFF: Place both fingers on the notes to be sounded. Strike the first note and without picking, pull the finger off to sound the second (lower) note.

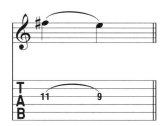

LEGATO SLIDE: Strike the first note and then slide the same fret-hand finger up or down to the second note. The second note is not struck.

SHIFT SLIDE: Same as legato slide, except the second note is struck.

TRILL: Very rapidly alternate between the notes indicated by continuously hammering on and pulling off.

TAPPING: Hammer ("tap") the fret indicated with the pick-hand index or middle finger and pull off to the note fretted by the fret hand.

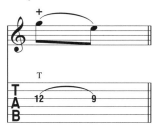

103

NATURAL HARMONIC: Strike the note while the fret-hand lightly touches the string directly over the fret indicated.

Harm.

12

PINCH HARMONIC: The note is fretted normally and a harmonic is produced by adding the edge of the thumb or the tip of the index finger of the pick hand to the normal pick attack.

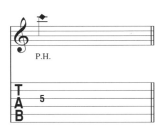

P.H.

5

HARP HARMONIC: The note is fretted normally and a harmonic is produced by gently resting the pick hand's index finger directly above the indicated fret (in parentheses) while the pick hand's thumb or pick assists by plucking the appropriate string.

H.H.

7(19)

PICK SCRAPE: The edge of the pick is rubbed down (or up) the string, producing a scratchy sound.

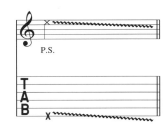

P.S.

MUFFLED STRINGS: A percussive sound is produced by laying the fret hand across the string(s) without depressing, and striking them with the pick hand.

PALM MUTING: The note is partially muted by the pick hand lightly touching the string(s) just before the bridge.

P.M. -------------

0   0   0   0

RAKE: Drag the pick across the strings indicated with a single motion.

rake - - -|

5
x
x

TREMOLO PICKING: The note is picked as rapidly and continuously as possible.

ARPEGGIATE: Play the notes of the chord indicated by quickly rolling them from bottom to top.

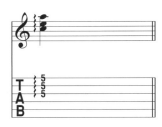

5
5
5

VIBRATO BAR DIVE AND RETURN: The pitch of the note or chord is dropped a specified number of steps (in rhythm), then returned to the original pitch.

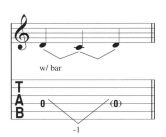

w/ bar

0   (0)

-1

VIBRATO BAR SCOOP: Depress the bar just before striking the note, then quickly release the bar.

w/ bar - - - - - - - - -|

4   5   7

VIBRATO BAR DIP: Strike the note and then immediately drop a specified number of steps, then release back to the original pitch.

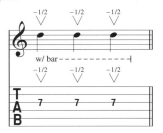

-1/2   -1/2   -1/2

w/ bar - - - - - - - - - -|

-1/2   -1/2   -1/2

7   7   7

Additional Musical Definitions

(accent)	• Accentuate note (play it louder).	
(accent)	• Accentuate note with great intensity.	
(staccato)	• Play the note short.	
⊓	• Downstroke	
∨	• Upstroke	
D.S. al Coda	• Go back to the sign (𝄋), then play until the measure marked "*To Coda*," then skip to the section labelled "**Coda**."	
D.C. al Fine	• Go back to the beginning of the song and play until the measure marked "*Fine*" (end).	

Rhy. Fig. • Label used to recall a recurring accompaniment pattern (usually chordal).

Riff • Label used to recall composed, melodic lines (usually single notes) which recur.

Fill • Label used to identify a brief melodic figure which is to be inserted into the arrangement.

Rhy. Fill • A chordal version of a Fill.

tacet • Instrument is silent (drops out).

• Repeat measures between signs.

• When a repeated section has different endings, play the first ending only the first time and the second ending only the second time.

NOTE: Tablature numbers in parentheses mean:
   1. The note is being sustained over a system (note in standard notation is tied), or
   2. The note is sustained, but a new articulation (such as a hammer-on, pull-off, slide or vibrato) begins, or
   3. The note is a barely audible "ghost" note (note in standard notation is also in parentheses).

HAL•LEONARD GUITAR PLAY•ALONG

This series will help you play your favorite songs quickly and easily. **INCLUDES TAB** Just follow the tab and listen to the CD to hear how the guitar should sound, and then play along using the separate backing tracks. Mac or PC users can also slow down the tempo without changing pitch by using the CD in their computer. The melody and lyrics are included in the book so that you can sing or simply follow along.

VOL. 1 – ROCK	00699570 / $16.99
VOL. 2 – ACOUSTIC	00699569 / $16.95
VOL. 3 – HARD ROCK	00699573 / $16.95
VOL. 4 – POP/ROCK	00699571 / $16.99
VOL. 5 – MODERN ROCK	00699574 / $16.99
VOL. 6 – '90s ROCK	00699572 / $16.99
VOL. 7 – BLUES	00699575 / $16.95
VOL. 8 – ROCK	00699585 / $14.95
VOL. 9 – PUNK ROCK	00699576 / $14.95
VOL. 10 – ACOUSTIC	00699586 / $16.95
VOL. 11 – EARLY ROCK	00699579 / $14.95
VOL. 12 – POP/ROCK	00699587 / $14.95
VOL. 13 – FOLK ROCK	00699581 / $14.95
VOL. 14 – BLUES ROCK	00699582 / $16.95
VOL. 15 – R&B	00699583 / $14.95
VOL. 16 – JAZZ	00699584 / $15.95
VOL. 17 – COUNTRY	00699588 / $15.95
VOL. 18 – ACOUSTIC ROCK	00699577 / $15.95
VOL. 19 – SOUL	00699578 / $14.95
VOL. 20 – ROCKABILLY	00699580 / $14.95
VOL. 21 – YULETIDE	00699602 / $14.95
VOL. 22 – CHRISTMAS	00699600 / $15.95
VOL. 23 – SURF	00699635 / $14.95
VOL. 24 – ERIC CLAPTON	00699649 / $16.95
VOL. 25 – LENNON & McCARTNEY	00699642 / $14.95
VOL. 26 – ELVIS PRESLEY	00699643 / $14.95
VOL. 27 – DAVID LEE ROTH	00699645 / $16.95
VOL. 28 – GREG KOCH	00699646 / $14.95
VOL. 29 – BOB SEGER	00699647 / $14.95
VOL. 30 – KISS	00699644 / $14.95
VOL. 31 – CHRISTMAS HITS	00699652 / $14.95
VOL. 32 – THE OFFSPRING	00699653 / $14.95
VOL. 33 – ACOUSTIC CLASSICS	00699656 / $16.95
VOL. 34 – CLASSIC ROCK	00699658 / $16.95
VOL. 35 – HAIR METAL	00699660 / $16.95
VOL. 36 – SOUTHERN ROCK	00699661 / $16.95
VOL. 37 – ACOUSTIC METAL	00699662 / $16.95
VOL. 38 – BLUES	00699663 / $16.95
VOL. 39 – '80s METAL	00699664 / $16.99
VOL. 40 – INCUBUS	00699668 / $17.95
VOL. 41 – ERIC CLAPTON	00699669 / $16.95
VOL. 42 – CHART HITS	00699670 / $16.95
VOL. 43 – LYNYRD SKYNYRD	00699681 / $17.95
VOL. 44 – JAZZ	00699689 / $14.95
VOL. 45 – TV THEMES	00699718 / $14.95

VOL. 46 – MAINSTREAM ROCK	00699722 / $16.95
VOL. 47 – HENDRIX SMASH HITS	00699723 / $19.95
VOL. 48 – AEROSMITH CLASSICS	00699724 / $16.99
VOL. 49 – STEVIE RAY VAUGHAN	00699725 / $16.95
VOL. 50 – NÜ METAL	00699726 / $14.95
VOL. 51 – ALTERNATIVE '90s	00699727 / $12.95
VOL. 52 – FUNK	00699728 / $14.95
VOL. 53 – DISCO	00699729 / $12.99
VOL. 54 – HEAVY METAL	00699730 / $14.95
VOL. 55 – POP METAL	00699731 / $14.95
VOL. 56 – FOO FIGHTERS	00699749 / $14.95
VOL. 57 – SYSTEM OF A DOWN	00699751 / $14.95
VOL. 58 – BLINK-182	00699772 / $14.95
VOL. 59 – GODSMACK	00699773 / $14.95
VOL. 60 – 3 DOORS DOWN	00699774 / $14.95
VOL. 61 – SLIPKNOT	00699775 / $14.95
VOL. 62 – CHRISTMAS CAROLS	00699798 / $12.95
VOL. 63 – CREEDENCE CLEARWATER REVIVAL	00699802 / $16.99
VOL. 64 – THE ULTIMATE OZZY OSBOURNE	00699803 / $16.99
VOL. 65 – THE DOORS	00699806 / $16.99
VOL. 66 – THE ROLLING STONES	00699807 / $16.95
VOL. 67 – BLACK SABBATH	00699808 / $16.99
VOL. 68 – PINK FLOYD – DARK SIDE OF THE MOON	00699809 / $16.99
VOL. 69 – ACOUSTIC FAVORITES	00699810 / $14.95
VOL. 70 – OZZY OSBOURNE	00699805 / $14.95
VOL. 71 – CHRISTIAN ROCK	00699824 / $14.95
VOL. 72 – ACOUSTIC '90S	00699827 / $14.95
VOL. 74 – PAUL BALOCHE	00699831 / $14.95
VOL. 75 – TOM PETTY	00699882 / $16.99
VOL. 76 – COUNTRY HITS	00699884 / $14.95
VOL. 78 – NIRVANA	00700132 / $14.95
VOL. 80 – ACOUSTIC ANTHOLOGY	00700175 / $19.95
VOL. 81 – ROCK ANTHOLOGY	00700176 / $22.99
VOL. 82 – EASY SONGS	00700177 / $12.99
VOL. 83 – THREE CHORD SONGS	00700178 / $12.99
VOL. 96 – THIRD DAY	00700560 / $14.95
VOL. 97 – ROCK BAND	00700703 / $14.99
VOL. 98 – ROCK BAND	00700704 / $14.95

Prices, contents, and availability subject to change without notice.

FOR MORE INFORMATION, SEE YOUR LOCAL MUSIC DEALER, OR WRITE TO:

HAL•LEONARD® CORPORATION
7777 W. BLUEMOUND RD. P.O. BOX 13819 MILWAUKEE, WI 53213

Visit Hal Leonard online at www.halleonard.com

Complete song lists available online.

0309

Get Better at Guitar

...with these Great Guitar Instruction Books from Hal Leonard!

101 GUITAR TIPS
INCLUDES TAB

STUFF ALL THE PROS KNOW AND USE

by Adam St. James

This book contains invaluable guidance on everything from scales and music theory to truss rod adjustments, proper recording studio set-ups, and much more. The book also features snippets of advice from some of the most celebrated guitarists and producers in the music business, including B.B. King, Steve Vai, Joe Satriani, Warren Haynes, Laurence Juber, Pete Anderson, Tom Dowd and others, culled from the author's hundreds of interviews.

00695737 Book/CD Pack..........................$16.95

AMAZING PHRASING
INCLUDES TAB

50 WAYS TO IMPROVE YOUR IMPROVISATIONAL SKILLS

by Tom Kolb

This book/CD pack explores all the main components necessary for crafting well-balanced rhythmic and melodic phrases. It also explains how these phrases are put together to form cohesive solos. Many styles are covered – rock, blues, jazz, fusion, country, Latin, funk and more – and all of the concepts are backed up with musical examples. The companion CD contains 89 demos for listening, and most tracks feature full-band backing.

00695583 Book/CD Pack..........................$19.95

BLUES YOU CAN USE
INCLUDES TAB

by John Ganapes

A comprehensive source designed to help guitarists develop both lead and rhythm playing. Covers: Texas, Delta, R&B, early rock and roll, gospel, blues/rock and more. Includes: 21 complete solos • chord progressions and riffs • turnarounds • moveable scales and more. CD features leads and full band backing.

00695007 Book/CD Pack..........................$19.95

FRETBOARD MASTERY
INCLUDES TAB

by Troy Stetina

Untangle the mysterious regions of the guitar fretboard and unlock your potential. *Fretboard Mastery* familiarizes you with all the shapes you need to know by applying them in real musical examples, thereby reinforcing and reaffirming your newfound knowledge. The result is a much higher level of comprehension and retention.

00695331 Book/CD Pack..........................$19.95

FRETBOARD ROADMAPS – 2ND EDITION

ESSENTIAL GUITAR PATTERNS THAT ALL THE PROS KNOW AND USE

by Fred Sokolow

The updated edition of this bestseller features more songs, updated lessons, and a full audio CD! Learn to play lead and rhythm anywhere on the fretboard, in any key; play a variety of lead guitar styles; play chords and progressions anywhere on the fretboard; expand your chord vocabulary; and learn to think musically – the way the pros do.

00695941 Book/CD Pack..........................$14.95

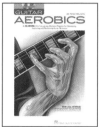

GUITAR AEROBICS
INCLUDES TAB

A 52-WEEK, ONE-LICK-PER-DAY WORKOUT PROGRAM FOR DEVELOPING, IMPROVING & MAINTAINING GUITAR TECHNIQUE

by Troy Nelson

From the former editor of *Guitar One* magazine, here is a daily dose of vitamins to keep your chops fine tuned! Musical styles include rock, blues, jazz, metal, country, and funk. Techniques taught include alternate picking, arpeggios, sweep picking, string skipping, legato, string bending, and rhythm guitar. These exercises will increase speed, and improve dexterity and pick- and fret-hand accuracy. The accompanying CD includes all 365 workout licks plus play-along grooves in every style at eight different metronome settings.

00695946 Book/CD Pack..........................$19.95

GUITAR CLUES
INCLUDES TAB

OPERATION PENTATONIC

by Greg Koch

Join renowned guitar master Greg Koch as he clues you in to a wide variety of fun and valuable pentatonic scale applications. Whether you're new to improvising or have been doing it for a while, this book/CD pack will provide loads of delicious licks and tricks that you can use right away, from volume swells and chicken pickin' to intervallic and chordal ideas. The CD includes 65 demo and play-along tracks.

00695827 Book/CD Pack..........................$19.95

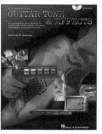

INTRODUCTION TO GUITAR TONE & EFFECTS

by David M. Brewster

This book/CD pack teaches the basics of guitar tones and effects, with audio examples on CD. Readers will learn about: overdrive, distortion and fuzz • using equalizers • modulation effects • reverb and delay • multi-effect processors • and more.

00695766 Book/CD Pack..........................$14.95

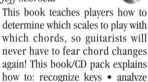

PICTURE CHORD ENCYCLOPEDIA

This comprehensive guitar chord resource for all playing styles and levels features five voicings of 44 chord qualities for all twelve keys – 2,640 chords in all! For each, there is a clearly illustrated chord frame, as well as *an actual photo* of the chord being played! Includes info on basic fingering principles, open chords and barre chords, partial chords and broken-set forms, and more.

00695224 ....$19.95

SCALE CHORD RELATIONSHIPS
INCLUDES TAB

by Michael Mueller & Jeff Schroedl

This book teaches players how to determine which scales to play with which chords, so guitarists will never have to fear chord changes again! This book/CD pack explains how to: recognize keys • analyze chord progressions • use the modes • play over nondiatonic harmony • use harmonic and melodic minor scales • use symmetrical scales such as chromatic, whole-tone and diminished scales • incorporate exotic scales such as Hungarian major and Gypsy minor • and much more!

00695563 Book/CD Pack..........................$14.95

SPEED MECHANICS FOR LEAD GUITAR
INCLUDES TAB

Take your playing to the stratosphere with the most advanced lead book by this proven heavy metal author. *Speed Mechanics* is the ultimate technique book for developing the kind of speed and precision in today's explosive playing styles. Learn the fastest ways to achieve speed and control, secrets to make your practice time really count, and how to open your ears and make your musical ideas more solid and tangible. Packed with over 200 vicious exercises including Troy's scorching version of "Flight of the Bumblebee." Music and examples demonstrated on CD. 89-minute audio.

00699323 Book/CD Pack..........................$19.95

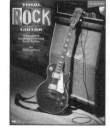

TOTAL ROCK GUITAR
INCLUDES TAB

A COMPLETE GUIDE TO LEARNING ROCK GUITAR

by Troy Stetina

This unique and comprehensive source for learning rock guitar is designed to develop both lead and rhythm playing. It covers: getting a tone that rocks • open chords, power chords and barre chords • riffs, scales and licks • string bending, strumming, palm muting, harmonics and alternate picking • all rock styles • and much more. The examples are in standard notation with chord grids and tab, and the CD includes full-band backing for all 22 songs.

00695246 Book/CD Pack..........................$19.99